The Book of Cricket Quotations

THE BOOK OF CRICKET QUOTATIONS

Peter Ball and David Hopps

Stanley Paul

LONDON   SYDNEY   AUCKLAND   JOHANNESBURG

Stanley Paul and Co. Ltd
An imprint of Random Century Group Ltd
20 Vauxhall Bridge Road, London SW1V 2SA

Random Century Australia (Pty) Ltd
20 Alfred Street, Milsons Point, Sydney, NSW 2061

Random Century New Zealand Limited
19 Archers Road, PO Box 40–086, Glenfield, Auckland 10

Century Hutchinson South Africa (Pty) Ltd
PO Box 337, Bergvlei 2012, South Africa

First published 1986
Revised edition 1990

Set in 10/11½pt Linotron Times
by Deltatype Ltd, Ellesmere Port, Cheshire

Printed and bound in Great Britain
by The Guernsey Press Co. Ltd, Guernsey, C.I.

British Library Cataloguing in Publication Data
The book of cricket quotations.
1. Cricket
I. Ball, Peter, *1943–*   II. Hopps, David
796.358
ISBN 0 09 174468 7

Contents

Acknowledgements

Cricket has a huge literature, much of it literary in the worst, most arch way possible. Only recently has it been tracked by an army of popular press journalists poised to snap up and record every word uttered by the main protagonists. And in the best English establishment traditions of secrecy, players' thoughts are carefully censored before they appear in print. Nevertheless, we have tried to capture the game's earthy realities, preferring a revealing comment in the heat of the moment to an erudite reflection from afar some time later. Therefore, our general thanks go to the journalists who know a good quote when they see one. Without them this book would lack what immediacy it has. We owe a more specific debt to Tony Woodhouse, for free access to his magnificent library of cricketana; and to all the publishers and authors who waived copyright so magnanimously, especially *The Cricketer* whose files proved a gold-mine. We have tried to be exact with our sources, although have also been anxious to avoid tedious repetition.

The authors and publishers would also like to thank the following for allowing the use of copyright photographs: Simon Bruty/All-Sport; Adrian Murrell/All-Sport; Patrick Eagar; Graeme Fowler; the Hulton–Deutsch Collection; Graham Morris; Sport and General.

Peter Ball
David Hopps

1
The Greats and Others

Players

Terry Alderman (Kent, Gloucestershire, Australia)

THATCHER Out
lbw Alderman 0

GRAFFITI in a London loo, **1989**.

ENGLAND'S problem is that they've treated Terry Alderman as an outswing bowler. Actually, he hasn't really swung it away much at all.

DEAN JONES, Alderman's Australian teammate, during 4–0 Ashes win in **1989**. Gooch and Co would disagree.

TERRY got a great deal of lbws in this series but most of them were taken with straight balls.

BOBBY SIMPSON, Australian team manager, during 1989 Ashes series.

Michael Atherton (Lancashire, England)

HE will go all the way in the game, but we couldn't put him in ahead of players who have lifted us up the table or those who have scored more than 700 runs in the second team.

DAVID HUGHES, Lancashire captain, explaining why Atherton was not in the Lancashire team in spite of coming down from Cambridge averaging 60.45 in **1988**.

Trevor Bailey (Essex, England)

SEEING Trevor Bailey prepare for a session in the field was like a lecture in anatomy.

RAY EAST, *A Funny Turn*, **1983**.

IT requires an earthquake to make him change his game in midstream.

DOUG INSOLE, *Cricket from the Middle*, **1960**.

S. F. Barnes (Staffordshire, Lancashire, England)

IF you wanted to score runs off Barnes, you had to score off good bowling.

LEARIE CONSTANTINE, after scoring 90 for Nelson *v* Rawtenstall when Barnes was 59.

AT least if we go down, we'll take that bugger Barnes down with us.

A. C. MACLAREN during a rough trip home from Australia, **1902**. MacLaren had picked Barnes from league cricket to make a tour.

Ken Barrington (Surrey, England)

WHENEVER I see Ken coming to the wicket, I imagine the Union Jack fluttering behind him.

WALLY GROUT, **1965**.

BARRINGTON was obviously not happy against the fast bowlers. Few batsmen are, but the majority hide their feelings. I think if I bowled to Barrington I should bowl a bouncer or two just to please my own ego, without having regard to the batsman's feelings.

W. E. BOWES on Second Test, England *v* S. Africa, **1960**.

Alec Bedser (Surrey, England)

ALEC rolled his fingers over the ball as he delivered it, and as it swung it pitched on the seam and became, as it were, a leg-spinner. As it hit the turf, it would cut away sharply.

GODFREY EVANS on Bedser's invention of the leg-cutter.

David Boon (Australia)

BOON appears a most contented cricketer. I can visualise him on a sheep farm in Tasmania, sipping lager on the verandah, the ideal temperament for dealing with fast bowlers.

SIR LEN HUTTON, **1985**.

Allan Border (Essex, Australia)

BORDER has not so much style as a *modus operandi*. He is utterly practical.

JOHN WOODCOCK, *The Times*, **1985**.

Ian Botham (Somerset, England)

THE first rock 'n' roll cricketer.

SIR LEN HUTTON, the *Observer*, **1986**.

I think if you made him Prime Minister tomorrow, he'd pick this country up in ten minutes.

BILL ALLEY, umpire, **1980**.

IAN Botham represents everything that's the best in Britain. He's Biggles, the VC, El Alamein, the tank commander, he's everything. I mean, how could a schoolboy not want to be like Ian Botham?

TIM HUDSON, Botham's agent, **1985**.

IN no way inhibited by any capacity to over-intellectualise. Repertoire of brilliantly witty party tricks includes pouring drinks down other players' girlfriends.

FRANCES EDMONDS, wife of England colleague Phil, in the *Daily Express*, **1985**.

HE doesn't give a damn; he wants to ride a horse, down a pint, roar around the land, waking up the sleepers, show them things can be done. As it is, he has to play cricket all the time and worry about newspapermen, a Gulliver tied down by the little people.

PETER ROEBUCK in *It Sort of Clicks*, Roebuck and Ian Botham, **1986**.

HE would probably not fit the bill as the schoolboy's vision of the dedicated superstar.

GRAHAM GOOCH, *Out of the Wilderness*, **1985**.

HE is the greatest match-winner the game has ever known.

MIKE BREARLEY, former England captain. **1985**.

HE couldn't bowl a hoop downhill.

F. S. TRUEMAN, **1985**.

HIS role in the side is now clear: he is not a hack bowler to be allowed to bowl all day: he is a striker, to be taken off quickly if he looks below par, but allowed a fair degree of leeway to experiment. We should have more trust in his flair, and his instinct for wangling wickets.

MIKE BREARLEY replying to criticism of Botham's bowling in **1985**.

HE must have put more backsides on seats than any other English cricketer since Denis Compton.

BOB TAYLOR, **1985**.

HE couldn't bat to save himself. I bowled to him with a dicky arm during the 1977 tour and he was either dropped four times or made nought.

JEFF THOMSON, Australian paceman, **1980**.

WHO writes your bloody scripts?

GRAHAM GOOCH to Ian Botham, who had just taken a wicket with his first delivery on returning to Test cricket after suspension, England *v* New Zealand, **1986**.

THE easiest job I ever had. Ian told me when he proposed to bowl – and when he was coming off.

JULIAN WYATT, Somerset Second XI captain, on finding Botham in his side after suspension, **1986**.

THERE were two or three who were adversely affected by Ian's presence. Ian gave 120 per cent on the field, but he only ever had 50 – 80 per cent of his ability to give because he was never fit. He turned up for training only a couple of times, and the coach, Ray Reynolds, said it was better he didn't come because he was a disruptive influence when he was there.

GREG CHAPPELL, Queensland selector and former Australian captain, on Queensland's decision to terminate Botham's contract in **1988**.

HE pushed me off a chair and wanted to continue to fight outside. Later he followed up with an empty beer glass in my face and told me he would cut me from ear to ear.

IAN CHAPPELL on the celebrated incident early in Botham's career.

I'VE been rooming with him all season and he's done no walking at all. Then he comes here and goes off, whoosh. The man's unbelievable. He's a freak.

GREG RITCHIE, Botham's flagging, fag-puffing Queensland team-mate, during the Hannibal crossing of the Alps, **1988**.

LES Anglais sont fous!

FRENCHMAN'S comment after witnessing Ian Botham's Hannibal trek across the Alps in aid of leukaemia research, **1988**.

IT'S not the fault of my cooking. He gets no potatoes, stodgy pudding or anything that's fattening. He simply hasn't played enough cricket. It's the weather.

KATHY, Botham's wife, **1981**, in response to criticism that Ian was overweight.

DON'T try to change him or the way he plays. Do that and you've lost your chance of winning Test matches.

KIM HUGHES, Australian captain, **1981**.

IAN is a man who is very warm in friendship, but very ugly in enmity.

PETER ROEBUCK on his former county colleague, **1988**.

So far as I know there has never been a St Ian. If ever one were to be created, I can't think it would be anything to do with Ian Terence Botham.

KATHY BOTHAM, after her husband confessed to smoking marijuana, **1986**.

No Iron Bottom?

PASSER-BY in Rawalpindi on Botham's absence from the England touring team, **1987**.

Geoffrey Boycott (Yorkshire, England)

Brighter Cricket With Geoff Boycott – No. 1: The Backward Defensive Stroke.

ILLUSTRATED COACHING SERIES (recorded by Mike Selvey, the *Guardian*, **1985).**

HE is of the type who are likely to have enjoyed quite a fill of wine, women and song.

FRASER WHITE, graphologist, analysing Boycott's handwriting in *The Cricketer*, **1975**.

As I stood at the non-striker's end, I felt a wave of admiration for my partner; wiry, slight, dedicated, a lonely man doing a lonely job all these years. What is it that compels Geoffrey Boycott to prove himself again and again among his peers?

MIKE BREARLEY, **1979**.

FOR a man with so much talent, I just feel it is sad that he is no longer willing to offer it. The difficult thing is how any player can lose his appetite to play for his country.

MIKE DENNESS, England captain, on Boycott's self-imposed Test exile, **1975**.

HIS ability to be where the fast bowlers aren't has long been a talking point among cricketers.

TONY GREIG, after Boycott turned down Packer offer, **1978**.

THE greatness of Boycott the batsman and the gaffes of Boycott the man had common roots in an unceasing quest after perfection to the nth degree.

FRANK TYSON, *The Test Within*, **1987**.

THE greatest tragedy of his troubled life is that, above all else, in the desire to be admired and loved by everyone, he has this enormous capacity for upsetting people.

TONY GREIG, **1983**.

I'VE been swamped by letters from ordinary Yorkshire members who can't contain their outrage. I've heard from others whose children won't stop crying because they'll never see Geoff bat again at Headingley.

SID FIELDEN, policeman, lay preacher and pro-Boycott organiser on Yorkshire committee, after the Yorkshire batsman's sacking, **1983**.

GEOFFREY Boycott is a very good batsman. I wish I had never met him.

SID FIELDEN, formerly Boycott's greatest ally on the Yorkshire committee, in **1985**.

THE best slow batsman in the world.

KEITH FLETCHER, England captain, when Boycott left India tour early because of illness, **1982**.

GEOFFREY Boycott is a giant playing among pygmies.

PETER BRIGGS, leader of Yorkshire Reform Group, **1981**.

IN attaining his world record Mr Boycott has occupied the creases of the world for 75 full days.

BILL FRINDALL, after Boycott had overtaken Sobers' Test aggregate record of 8032 runs in New Delhi.

WE sometimes argue about the cricketer we would choose to bat for one's life (consensus answer: Don Bradman for your life, Geoff Boycott for his own).

MATTHEW ENGEL, the *Guardian*, **1989**.

I'VE just been sat outside and you can absolutely feel it. There are people holding their hearts when he plays a shot. The one he hit in the air over there, there was two chaps at the side of me who nearly passed out.

FRED TRUEMAN's BBC radio commentary, Headingley Test between England and Australia, **1977**. Geoffrey Boycott is about to complete his 100th hundred. (From *The Ashes: Highlights since 1948*, 1989.)

IT's not an end to my ambition. I haven't played for England a third time yet.

BOYCOTT, after scoring his 150th first-class century against Leicestershire, June **1986**.

HIS attention to the practical detail of equipment and the minutiae of every stroke has probably never been rivalled.

FRANK TYSON, *The Test Within*, **1987**.

You are my hero. I don't care what they say.

CUSTOMS MAN at Trinidad airport. Boycott spent 18 hours under close arrest after arriving without a valid work permit – and South African connections, **1986**.

Sir Don Bradman (Australia)

THERE's no ruddy best ball to bowl at the Don.

BILL VOCE, **1933**.

BRADMAN was a team in himself. I think the Don was too good: he spoilt the game. He got too many runs. The pot calling the kettle black? No, I was human; he got hundreds every time he went in. . . . He was mechanical; he was the greatest run-getting machine of all time. I do not think we want to see another one quite like him. I do not think we ever shall.

JACK HOBBS, *The Times*, **1952**.

FEW will be found to admit that the hero-worship, almost amounting to idolatry, to which, for example, Bradman was subject, is desirable for the game's good.

DOUGLAS JARDINE, **1933**.

No one ever laughed about Bradman. He was no laughing matter.

R. C. ROBERTSON-GLASGOW.

BRADMAN was the summing up of the Efficient Age which succeeded the Golden Age. Here was brilliance safe and sure, streamlined and without impulse. Victor Trumper was the flying bird; Bradman the aeroplane.

NEVILLE CARDUS, *Autobiography*, **1947**.

EACH slow mouthful was an essay in methods of digestion, in relaxation, in cold planning and contemplation of the real feast ahead.

JACK FINGLETON on Bradman's lunch-hour eating manner.

HOLLIES pitches the ball up slowly and . . . he's bowled . . .
Bradman bowled Hollies nought . . . bowled Hollies nought . . .
and what do you say under these circumstances? How . . . I wonder
if you see the ball very clearly in your last Test in England, on a
ground where you've played some of the biggest cricket of your life
and where the opposing side has just stood around you and given
you three cheers, and the crowd has clapped you all the way to the
wicket. I wonder if you see the ball at all.

JOHN ARLOTT's commentary on BBC radio at The Oval, **1948**. Don Bradman, in his
last Test, was bowled second ball, for nought, by a googly from Eric Hollies.

WHAT makes you think I would only have maintained my average?
If I'd had the opportunity of playing in India, Pakistan and Sri
Lanka, I think I might have increased it.

SIR DON BRADMAN on being told in **1988** that had he played as many games as Sunil
Gavaskar did to amass his Test record aggregate, at his 99.94 average he would
have virtually doubled Gavaskar's total.

Ian Chappell (Australia)

CHAPPELL was a coward. He needed a crowd around him before he
would say anything. He was sour like milk that had been sitting in
the sun for a week.

IAN BOTHAM in *It Sort of Clicks*, Botham and Peter Roebuck, **1986**.

William Clarke (Founder of the All England XI)

EXCEPTING his own faults, Clarke knew more than any man alive
about cricket.

GEORGE PARR (quoted in E. W. Swanton's revision of H. S. Altham, *A History of
Cricket*), **1962**.

Brian Close (Yorkshire, Somerset, England)

In future, I shall always be able to tell when the cricket season begins. All I have to do is to listen to the sound of Brian Close being hit by a cricket ball.

ERIC MORECAMBE, comedian, after Close withstood West Indian bumper barrage on his return to Test cricket, **1976**.

Denis Compton (Middlesex, England)

I wouldn't say I coached him, but I didn't mess him up.

GEORGE FENNER, head coach at Lord's, on his early coaching of Compton, **1958**.

He was the only player to call his partner for a run and wish him good luck at the same time.

JOHN WARR, his Middlesex colleague, in *The Cricketer*.

I was as fit as a flea; I did what came naturally and I enjoyed myself.

COMPTON, explaining his summer of **1947**, which brought 3816 first-class runs and 18 centuries.

The facet of his cricket which went to the heart of the average club player who watched him was his improvisation, which rectified such error as, in ordinary men, would be fatal.

JOHN ARLOTT, *Vintage Summer: 1947*.

If my mother hadn't thrown my football boots on the fire, I might have become as famous as Denis Compton.

LEN HUTTON.

Denis Compton and Bill Edrich (Middlesex, England)

COMPTON and Edrich are of the happy philosophy which keeps failure in its place by laughter, like boys who fall on an ice slide and rush back to try it again.

R. C. ROBERTSON-GLASGOW, *Wisden*, **1948**.

Learie Constantine (West Indies)

HE revolted against the revolting contrast between his first-class status as a cricketer and his third-class status as a man.

C. L. R. JAMES, *Beyond a Boundary*, **1963**.

Martin Crowe (Somerset, New Zealand)

HE won't be great until he stops being a perfectionist and starts mutilating the bowlers.

IAN BOTHAM in *It Sort of Clicks*, Botham and Peter Roebuck, **1986**.

Phil DeFreitas (Leicestershire, Lancashire, England)

HE bowls too many wicket-taking balls.

MICKY STEWART, England team manager, analysing DeFreitas' bowling problems in **1988**. Test statistics hardly bore out his theory.

Mike Denness (Kent, Essex, England)

To dismiss this lad Denness you don't have to bowl fast. You just have to run up fast.

BRIAN CLOSE, **1974**.

Ted Dexter (Sussex, England)

ERROL Holmes is called 'the last of the dandies' – yet Dexter is seen as a possible successor. Does a dandy chew gum? Who knows – nowadays?

G. D. MARTINEAU, *The Cricketer*.

Graham Dilley (Kent, England)

COWANS should remember what happened to Graham Dilley, who started off as a genuinely quick bowler. Then they started stuffing 'line and length' into his ear, and now he has Dennis Lillee's action with Denis Thatcher's pace.

GEOFFREY BOYCOTT, **1982**.

J. W. H. T. Douglas (Essex, England)

HE has earned great fame as a boxer, and in the ring his quickness of foot is exceptional; but at cricket his boots always seem too big for him and too heavy.

THE CRICKETER, 'Portrait of Douglas', **1921**.

Ray East (Essex)

HIS epitaph will be the stories he created, stories which became bar-room legends around the cricket circuit. Cricketers swap Ray East experiences rather as some people swap Irish jokes.

GRAHAM GOOCH, East's Essex colleague, in *Out of the Wilderness*, **1985**.

Bill Edrich (Middlesex, England)

EVEN today with those artificial hips and at the age of 70, wouldn't he still be more of a success in the West Indies than some of the snivelling, long-haired, money-conscious yobbos who now represent England?

JOHN JUNOR, *Sunday Express*, **1986**.

Phil Edmonds (Middlesex, England)

REPUTATION for being arrogant and awkward, probably because he *is* arrogant and awkward. Works very hard at trying to be controversial and iconoclastic, but basically a pillar of the establishment.

FRANCES EDMONDS, *Daily Express*, **1985**.

PHIL Edmonds needs two more field changes to get his 1000 for the season.

JIM LAKER, **1985**.

I just have to make a *suggestion* these days and it is interpreted as being antagonistic.

PHIL EDMONDS, **1984**.

John Emburey (Middlesex, England)

I could never be a 100 per cent professional like John Emburey.

PHIL EDMONDS, his Middlesex and England spin colleague, **1982**.

I'M not a flighty bowler. I like to use my control to put pressure on the batsman, react to what he does and force him into error. And my bowling doesn't really change. So I'm not so good at exploiting a bad wicket; I'm a hard-wicket bowler.

JOHN EMBUREY.

A conversation with him would be 50 per cent shorter if he deleted the expletives.

MIKE SELVEY, **1985**.

C. B. Fry (Surrey, Sussex, Hampshire)

HE was one of the last of his kind – and certainly the finest specimen of it – the amateurs, the smiling gentlemen of games, intensely devoted to the skill and the struggle but always with a certain gaiety, romantic at heart but classical in style.

J. B. PRIESTLEY, *The English*, **1973**.

Joel Garner (Somerset, West Indies)

BLIMEY, the bugger can't bend as well can he?

BRIAN CLOSE, **1977**.

Mike Gatting (Middlesex, England)

HE was a hyperactive little menace, but when he got hold of a cricket bat he was a different person – the bat was his mate, his best friend.

SHEILA SUMNER on the boy Gatt at Brondesbury CC, in *Leading from the Front*, **1988**.

'Do you want Gatt a foot wider?'
'No. He'd burst.'

EXCHANGE between David Gower and Chris Cowdrey, the bowler, during the Third Test, India *v* England, Calcutta, **1985**.

David Gower (Leicestershire, England)

DIFFICULT to be more laid back without being actually comatose.

FRANCES EDMONDS, *Daily Express*, **1985**.

PERHAPS Gower will eventually realise cricket's not always about champagne. It's a bread and butter game.

BRIAN BRAIN, Gloucestershire seamer, *Another Day, Another Match*, **1981**.

HAS been known to enjoy a glass of red wine as long as it is vintage, and worth not less than £150 a bottle.

JON AGNEW, *8 Days a Week*, **1988**.

E. M. Grace (Gloucestershire, England)

E.M. was a coroner, but I shouldn't like anyone to hold an inquest on his cricket.

W. G. GRACE on his brother.

THE stir that E.M. made was all the greater because of the scandalous manner in which he outraged every law of batting that had hitherto been held sacred.

BERNARD DARWIN, *W. G. Grace*, **1934**.

EARLIEST, and not least famous of Cowshotters.

A. C. M. CROOME.

'UNCLE Ted's' proximity to the batsman, apart from the chances of a catch, was no inconceivable asset to the bowler. He kept up a running commentary with the batsman, which, in the case of some, was apt to prevent that entire concentration of thought which is so requisite for success.

G. L. JESSOP, in *The Cricketer*. 'Uncle Ted' was Grace the elder's nickname.

W. G. Grace (Gloucestershire, England)

HE revolutionized cricket. He turned it from an accomplishment into a science.

RANJITSINHJI, *The Jubilee Book of Cricket*, **1897**.

WHAT W.G. did was to unite in his mighty self all the good points of all the good players, and to make utility the criterion of style.

RANJITSINHJI, *The Jubilee Book of Cricket*, **1897**.

HE turned the old one-stringed instrument into a many chorded lyre. But in addition he made his execution equal his invention.

RANJITSINHJI, *The Jubilee Book of Cricket*, **1897**.

W.G.'s name will not be associated with any one stroke because, when he was physically in his prime, he played them all at least as well as the specialists. Even when he was fat and heavy-footed he made a thousand runs in May largely by pulling the ball powerfully and for longer periods than his brother E.M. ever could.

A. C. M. CROOME.

ADMISSION 3d; If Dr W.G. plays, Admission 6d.

NOTICE outside grounds in **1870s**.

I call him a nonsuch; he ought to be made to play with a littler bat.

TOM EMMETT, of Yorkshire, after W. G. Grace hit a century for South *v* North at Sheffield, quoted in Lord Hawke's *Recollections and Reminiscences,* **1922**.

IT's Grace before meat, Grace after dinner and Grace all the time.

TOM EMMETT.

THE first ball I sent whizzing through his whiskers; after that he kept hitting me off his blinkin' ear'ole for 4.

ERNEST JONES, Australia, on a game *v* Lord Sheffield's XI, **1896**.

IT ain't a bit of use my bowling good 'uns to him now; it's a case of I put the ball where I please and he puts it where he pleases.

JEMMY SHAW, Notts fast bowler, brought on when W. G. Grace was well set, **1870s**.

I always thought the old man depended rather too much on the umpires for leg before. . . .

LORD HARRIS, *Wisden,* **1896**.

WHAT, are you going, Doctor? There's still one stump standing.

CHARLES KORTRIGHT, Essex pace bowler, to W. G. Grace after bowling him.

ONE of the dirtiest necks I ever kept wicket behind.

LORD COBHAM.

Tom Graveney (Gloucestershire, Worcestershire, England)

HE played for Gloucestershire, he works for us.

LEN COLDWELL, Worcestershire team-mate, on Graveney's change of attitude, **1966**.

David Green (Lancashire, Gloucestershire)

IF ever there was a larger-than-life guy, it was Greeny; extremely intelligent and witty, he had an old-fashioned attitude to new-fangled things such as training and fitness programmes. He didn't believe in them. For him, cricket was a way of making a lot of friends, knocking the cover off the ball if possible and making regular attempts to boost the profits of certain breweries.

MIKE PROCTER, in *Mike Procter and Cricket*, **1981**.

Clarrie Grimmett (Australia)

ONE of the gentlest bowlers ever to lift a ball, he walked gently, picked up a cup of tea gently, arranged his tie with whispering fingers. His cap was set as though with a spirit level – none of this Yorkshire tilt for the fastidious Mr Grimmett.

ARTHUR MAILEY, *10 for 66 and All That*, **1958**.

Wally Grout (Australia)

IF you threw a ball to Wally Grout a bit off target you'd get the full treatment. One hell of a glare and something like: 'These hands are my life, protect them!'

NEIL HAWKE, **1972**.

William Gunn (Nottinghamshire)

I felt tired of cricket perhaps once – when I listened to Billy Gunn saying 'No!' at Lord's for seven and a half hours.

SYDNEY GREGORY on Gunn's 228 for Players *v* Australia, Lord's **1890**.

Richard Hadlee (Nottinghamshire, New Zealand)

ON the field his approach is calculating, commercial, bloodless, too much the chartered accountant to be heroic.

SCYLD BERRY, the *Observer*, **1988**.

HE describes himself humbly as 'basically a line-length, control bowler'. This utterly conceals his method, which is to expose a batsman's frailties as quickly as possible using considerable variety, but within a framework of almost monotonous accuracy. The feeling of despair that he inflicts on a suddenly scoreless batsman is emulated only by Derek Underwood of modern bowlers.

SIMON HUGHES, Middlesex seam bowler, **1988**.

[HE] propelled the fastest bouncer I have ever received. How it did not decapitate me I will never know. He followed it up with a brilliantly concealed slower ball which I was convinced was destined for my throat until it suddenly dipped and struck me on the foot. His secret is his action, which is faultless and almost robotically repetitive, regardless of the speed or length of delivery. He is a brilliant con-man.

SIMON HUGHES.

IF he has a weakness, it's against left-handers when he has to bowl over the wicket at them – he's got such a grooved, off-stump line at right-handers that he finds it difficult to change. He's also got this ability to make right-handers play at width, to chase the ball they don't have to play. 'Both' used to have that sort of magnetism.

BRUCE FRENCH, Nottinghamshire wicket-keeper, **1988**.

IT was like batting against the World XI at one end and Ilford Second XI at the other.

ANONYMOUS ENGLAND BATSMAN on Hadlee and his New Zealand colleagues' bowling in the Lord's Test, **1986**.

Wes Hall (West Indies)

IT was the first time two batsmen have ever crossed in the toilet.

TONY LEWIS, facing Wes Hall, the West Indian pace bowler, for the first time, Glamorgan *v* West Indies, **1963**.

Wally Hammond (Gloucestershire, England)

WE Australians heard that Wally Hammond was very weak on the legside, that he was solely an offside batsman. Very well, we bowled outside the leg to keep him quiet or tease him into doing something desperate. Clarrie Grimmett, the arch conspirator, with sinister intent at Adelaide pegged away a foot or two outside Wally's leg-stump waiting patiently for the great batsman to make a wild, uncharacteristic swing and be caught in front of the ladies' stand. Nothing happened. The ladies went on knitting or shelling peas for hubby's dinner. Clarrie, with that fastidious judgement few bowlers possess, sent down a ball in line with leg-stump. Almost simultaneously the ball crashed into the cover fence under the scoreboard.

ARTHUR MAILEY.

David Harris (Hambledon, All England)

HIS attitude, when preparing to deliver the ball, was masculine, erect and appalling. First he stood like a soldier at drill, upright. Then with a graceful and elegant curve, he raised the fatal ball to his forehead, and drawing back his right foot, started off. Woe to the unlucky wight who did not know how to stop these cannonades! His fingers would be ground to dust against the bat, his bones pulverised, and his blood scattered over the field. . . . Harris was terribly afflicted with the gout; it was at length difficult for him to stand, a great armchair was always brought into the field, and after the delivery of the ball, the hero sat down in his own calm and simple grandeur, and reposed.

REV. JOHN MITFORD on Hambledon's fast bowler, *Gentleman's Magazine*, **1833**.

Tom Hayward (Surrey)

HE was my greatest bugbear. He was what may be called a 'flat-catching' bowler. He looked so much simpler than he really was. Over confidence rather than diffidence of my ability to cope with him usually upset my applecart, for I could never rid myself of the conviction that in almost every ball there lurked a half-volley.

G. L. JESSOP.

George Hirst (Yorkshire, England)

How the devil can you play a ball that comes at you like a hard throw-in from cover-point?

S. M. J. WOODS on Hirst's bowling.

I have tossed my slow tripe at you till I grew weary, and I longed for the shades of eve. There was no man I would rather have made 50 off than you; no man I was more pleased to get out.

D. L. A. JEPHSON ('the Lob-ster'), tribute on Hirst's 50th birthday.

Sir Jack Hobbs (Surrey, England)

IT were impossible to fault him. He got 'em on good 'uns, he got 'em on bad 'uns, he got 'em on sticky 'uns, he got 'em on t'mat, against South African googlers, and he got 'em all over t'world.

WILFRED RHODES.

A professional who bats exactly like an amateur.

SIR PELHAM WARNER.

OTHERS scored faster; hit the ball harder; more obviously murdered bowling. No one else, though, ever batted with more consummate skill.

JOHN ARLOTT, *Jack Hobbs: Profile of The Master*, **1981**.

HE could have made 400 centuries – and if he'd played for Yorkshire he would have done.

WILFRED RHODES (Hobbs made 197, the most in cricket history).

Michael Holding (Lancashire, Derbyshire, West Indies)

A perfect running specimen, but I don't go to a Test to see running; if I wished to see that I would go to Crystal Palace to see Coe and Ovett.

JACK FINGLETON in *Batting from Memory*, **1981**.

WHISPERING Death.

HOLDING's nickname on the cricket circuit.

Sir Len Hutton (Yorkshire, England)

I am only setting up these records for Hutton to break them.

HERBERT SUTCLIFFE, Yorkshire batsman.

THERE'S nothing we can teach this lad.

GEORGE HIRST, Yorkshire coach, on Hutton's first appearance at county nets, **1930**.

HUTTON was never dull. His bat was part of his nervous system. His play was sculptured. His forward defensive stroke was a complete statement.

HAROLD PINTER, *Cricket '72*, **1972**.

UNLIKE Boycott, he could make the forward defensive look attractive.

TREVOR BAILEY in *The Ashes: Highlights Since 1948*, **1989**.

Merv Hughes (Australia)

IN cricket he was, from the beginning, the very model of the modern Australian fast bowler, a caricature that was big, bad and ugly. He scowled and cursed and was, accordingly, liked by the punters, who were in urgent need of a character. Being colourful and bad, Hughes filled a gap. No one pretended he was brilliant; on the contrary his build, manner and action scorned the idea. He was an ordinary bloke trying to make good without ever losing the air of a fellow with a hangover. But he was game, had the courage of a lion and the heart of an oak. Few took him seriously.

PETER ROEBUCK, *Sunday Times*, on Hughes before the West Indies' tour of Australia **1988–9**.

NOT the sort of quickish bowler who, upon being insulted, will issue a writ for libel. To the contrary, his handlebar moustache would bristle and he'd invite you for fisticuffs behind the pavilion. He'd been picked to mix it, so he did. By giving as good as he got, by being noisy, energetic and unrelenting, Hughes set the tone for Australia's fight-back.

PETER ROEBUCK as Hughes took five for 130 *v* West Indies, first innings, Second Test, Perth, **1988**.

Ray Illingworth (Yorkshire, England)

THE trouble with Illy is that he always wants his own way.

BRIAN CLOSE (who also did).

Imran Khan (Sussex, Pakistan)

I think he's a snob. He doesn't mix. And he gets very angry and picks on players for no reason.

QASIM OMAR, **1987**. Qasim had made drug allegations against international cricketers.

A Pathan with the Khan genes has a vengeful fire in his belly. They also keep their eye on the ball.

JONAH BARRINGTON, former squash champion. (Source: Frank Keating, the *Guardian*, **1987**.)

Sir F. S. Jackson (Yorkshire, England)

As I looked down on the vast congregation of cricketers who had known him, I could see from the rapt expression on their faces how they felt towards the great man . . . how they revered him; how indeed they reverenced him as though he were the Almighty, but infinitely stronger on the legside.

ASCRIBED BY GEORGE COX to the bishop delivering Jackson's funeral oration.

Kevin Jarvis (Kent)

IF I could bowl at myself, I would be very keen. It would be an amputation job to get the ball out of my hands.

KEVIN JARVIS, who averaged 3.15 with the bat in **1985**, after preventing Agnew claiming all ten wickets.

G. L. Jessop (Gloucestershire, England)

JESSOP was a terror. We reckoned in this game we'd make him go and fetch 'em. So we bowled wide on the offside. He fetched 'em all right. He went off like a spring-trap and, before you'd seen his feet move, he was standing on the offside of his stumps, pulling 'em over the square-leg boundary.

WILFRED RHODES on Jessop's century in each innings for Gloucestershire against Yorkshire, **1900**, quoted by A. A. Thomson, *Hirst and Rhodes*.

No man has ever driven a ball so hard, so high, and so often in so many different directions.

C. B. FRY on 'The Croucher'.

His speed of foot and eye and judgement, his strength of wrist, his timing and daring, all made him the most dangerous batsman the world will ever see; he didn't go in for huge hits; he made boundaries out of balls that the best batsmen would be content just to play.

S. M. J. WOODS, *The Cricketer*.

Jim Laker (Surrey, England)

No bugger ever got all ten when I was at the other end.

SYDNEY BARNES, after watching Jim Laker take all ten wickets for England *v* Australia, Old Trafford, **1956**.

David 'Syd' Lawrence (Gloucestershire, England)

HE tears in whether he's taken none for 100 or five for 30. The only thing worrying me about Syd playing for England is that he may try to run in so fast that he won't be able to let go of the ball.

DAVID GRAVENEY, Gloucestershire captain, on his fast bowler's international prospects, **1988**.

RATHER like facing up to a raging bull. The refined run-up still has a disconcerting chicane in it, there is a lot of puffing and blowing, a grimace or two, a huge leap and some serious pace to follow.

SIMON HUGHES, Middlesex seam bowler.

John Lever (Essex, England)

THERE must be a million stories about John Lever and at least one of them is printable.

ALLAN BORDER, Foreword to *Lever: A Cricketer's Cricketer*, **1989**.

Dennis Lillee and Jeff Thomson (Australia)

ASHES to ashes, dust to dust – If Thomson don't get ya, Lillee must. . . .

SYDNEY TELEGRAPH cartoon caption, **1975**.

THERE'S no batsman on earth who goes out to meet Dennis Lillee and Jeff Thomson with a smile on his face.

CLIVE LLOYD, **1975**.

I don't really like the new Dennis Lillee. There's no substitute for bowling fast and being able to make the good players jump.

DENNIS LILLEE, *My Life in Cricket,* **1982**, after his back injury had forced him to substitute skill for speed.

A great fast bowler, the best I have ever seen and one of the finest of all time. He had everything: courage, variety, high morale, arrogance, supreme fitness and aggression . . . but I am afraid I will also remember him as the bloke who stopped playing for love of the game and his country and started playing for money and to please the TV producers.

BOB WILLIS, *The Cricket Revolution,* **1981**.

IT'LL be all right if Dennis gets wickets, but if he doesn't the knockers will say 'silly old bastard'.

JEFF THOMSON on his former partner's decision to return to first-class cricket in **1988**.

Ray Lindwall (Australia)

HE was a great man at a party, and played his part in ensuring that no English brewery went out of business through lack of patronage.

JIM LAKER, *Over to Me,* **1960**.

George Macaulay (Yorkshire, 1920s)

THERE's only one man made more appeals than you, George, and that was Dr Barnardo.

BILL REEVE, umpire.

Stan McCabe (Australia)

COME and see this. Don't miss a minute of it. You'll never see the likes of this again.

DON BRADMAN to Australian side during Stan McCabe's 232 *v* England at Trent Bridge, **1938**.

Ken Mackay (Australia)

HE is the only athlete I have ever known who, as he walked, sagged at ankles, knees and hips.

JOHN ARLOTT, *The Cricketer*, **1963**.

Arthur Mailey (Australia)

IF Arthur Mailey was not cricket's greatest bowler, he was its greatest philosopher.

BEN TRAVERS, **1967**.

Philip Mead (Hampshire, England)

I wonder if there has been another player who understood the science of batsmanship as much as Mead.

HERBERT SUTCLIFFE.

HE pervaded a cricket pitch. He occupied it and encamped on it. He erected a tent with a system of infallible pegging, then posted inexorable sentries. He took guard with the air of a guest who, having been offered a weekend by his host, obstinately decides to reside for six months.

R. C. ROBERTSON-GLASGOW.

MEAD, you've been in five hours and you've just stonewalled.

R. W. V. ROBINS to Mead, when he had made 218 not out in five hours *v* Middlesex.

HELLO, Mead, I saw your father play in 1911.

AUSTRALIAN, mistakenly, to Mead, who toured Australia with MCC in **1911** and **1928**.

Colin Milburn (Northamptonshire, England)

I'VE always been a slogger and my father was a slogger before me.

COLIN MILBURN, **1966**.

Arthur Mold (Lancashire, 1880s)

PERSONALLY Mold was the nicest of men, and I am certain he never intentionally threw.

PELHAM WARNER. Mold bowled fast off six paces, and was no-balled 16 times in 10 overs for throwing against Somerset at Old Trafford.

Alfred Mynn (Kent, 1840s)

WITH his tall and stately presence, with his nobly moulded form,
His broad hand was ever open, his brave heart was ever warm.
All were proud of him, all loved him. As the changing seasons pass,
As our champion lies a-sleeping underneath the Kentish grass,
Proudly, sadly will we name him – to forget him were a sin.
Lightly lie the turf upon thee, kind and manly Alfred Mynn!

WILLIAM JEFFREY PROWSE, 'In Memoriam, Alfred Mynn', last verse.

Mudassar Nazar (Pakistan)

THEN there was that dark horse with the golden arm, Mudassar Nazar.

TREVOR BAILEY, BBC Test Match Special.

Philip Newport (Worcestershire, England)

To the best of my knowledge no bowler has ever arrived among the truly greats who transfers the ball from hand to hand during his run-up.

ROBIN MARLAR, 1988.

Bill O'Reilly (Australia)

WHEN bowling, he completely dominated the situation. He roared at umpires and scowled at batsmen. There was no sign of veneer or camouflage when he appealed, nor were there any apologies or beg pardons when the umpire indicated that the batsmen's legs were yards out of line with the stumps.

ARTHUR MAILEY.

To hit him for four would usually arouse a belligerent ferocity which made you sorry. It was almost like disturbing a hive of bees. He seemed to attack from all directions.

SIR DON BRADMAN, *Farewell to Cricket*, **1950**.

His googly was harder to spot than a soda-fountain in the bush.

COLIN MCCOOL, *Cricket is a Game*, **1961**.

Cecil Parkin (Lancashire, England)

HE took 14 wickets in the match. He bowled every possible variety of ball from fast-medium away swingers to the highest of full-tosses; he swung it both ways, he spun like a top, producing out of the hat leg-break, off-break, top-spinner and googly, with an occasional straight ball for good measure.

C. S. MARRIOTT on Parkin's 14 wickets *v* Yorkshire, in *The Complete Leg-Break Bowler*.

HAD it been possible, he would have bowled more than six different balls per over. In his continual startling variations of pace he actually gave the illusion, at the end of one over, of having brought his right hand over empty and served up a lob with his left. In another, he played the farcical trick when he suddenly stopped dead three yards behind the bowling crease and delivered a high, slow donkey-drop which, of all people, foxed out George Hirst.

C. S. MARRIOTT.

George Parr (Nottinghamshire, 1840s)

THERE is a tree at Nottingham which is, or was, known as George Parr's tree. It was situated at square leg, and it was his particular delight to hit over this bramble. All I can say is that the bowlers who gave him this particular ball were silly asses; no one supposed to be a bowler had any right to indulge the said veteran.

SAMMY WOODS.

Ted Peate (Yorkshire, England, 1880s)

ONE of my saddest tasks was to dismiss him from the Yorkshire eleven. But he bore me no grudge, and whenever I subsequently ran across him, invariably he greeted me with the old familiar smile and the same slow, spontaneous: 'Good morning, my Lord, I hope you are as well as I am.'

LORD HAWKE, *Recollections and Reminiscences*, **1924.**

Fuller Pilch (Kent, 1830s)

THEY may call it Pilch's 'poke' if they please, but I rather fancy that Pilch's 'poke' would puzzle some of our present-day bowlers. If a 'poke' means smothering the ball before it has time to rise and break, and placing it to the off or on with the greatest apparent ease, I shall much like to see it done again in these days.

FRED GALE, *The Game of Cricket*, **1870.**

Derek Pringle (Essex, England)

FAST bowlers wearing ear-rings?

FRED TRUEMAN, on Pringle's Test debut, **1982.**

Mike Procter (Gloucestershire, South Africa)

THE amazing thing about Procter is that he goes out with any bat he picks up; he never worries about the weight, balance or pick-up of a bat; he just goes out there and hammers it.

BRIAN BRAIN, **1979.**

Sonny Ramadhin (West Indies)

LIKE trying to play a boonch of confetti.

ASCRIBED TO a Derbyshire batsman by Ian Peebles, *Batter's Castle*, **1958.**

ALL you see is a blur of black hand, a white shirt with sleeves buttoned down to the wrist and a red blur.

DENIS COMPTON'S advice on Ramadhin to Keith Miller, **1951**.

Derek Randall (Nottinghamshire, England)

HE is the oddest mixture of uncertainty and hectic over-confidence. Somewhere between the two, and especially when his side is in peril, he is a balanced, shrewd player; a natural batsman whose judgement is reliable; his defence sound; his strokes flowingly appropriate to the ball bowled.

JOHN ARLOTT, **1983**.

Ranjitsinhji (Sussex, England, 1900s)

'E never played a Christian stroke in his life.

TED WAINWRIGHT, of Yorkshire. (Source: Cardus.)

THE coming of Ranji rather upset the 'off theory' business.

G. L. JESSOP.

AFTER being warned for years of the danger of playing back on a fast wicket, and especially to fast bowling, it came as rather a surprise to see the great Indian batsman transgressing against a principle so firmly fixed in one's mind.

G. L. JESSOP.

To attribute the two-shouldered stance to his wonderful leg-glides is absurd. To begin with he did not put his left leg on the on-side, as so many modern players do in attempting this stroke, but placed his left leg across his right leg on the off-side of the wicket, and at the same time deflected the ball with the turn of his wrists at the moment of impact.

SIR PELHAM WARNER, *The Cricketer*, **1923**.

Ian Redpath (Australia)

HE is everything most Australians are not . . . a model of batting technique.

RAY ILLINGWORTH, **1972**.

Viv Richards (Somerset, West Indies)

INSPIRED by a mixture of pride and prejudice.

FRANK TYSON, *The Test Within*, **1987**.

YOU may say he is a murderer with the bat. Well, if that is so, I'm a hooligan.

IAN BOTHAM in *It Sort of Clicks*, Botham and Peter Roebuck, **1986**.

Wilfred Rhodes (Yorkshire, England)

WHEN George [Hirst] got you out, you were out. When Wilfred got you out, you were out twice, because he knew by then how to get you out in the second innings too.

ROY KILNER, Yorkshire team-mate.

WILFRED studied the game more than a financier ever studied the stock market.

BILL BOWES, *Express Deliveries*, **1949**.

WILFRED couldn't see the stumps at my end. I could have been no more than a blurred and distant image, yet, bowling from memory, with his arm upright, he flighted the ball beautifully and dropped on a good length six times out of six. I played through a maiden over on merit and was glad enough to survive it.

BRIAN SELLERS, describing Rhodes' near-blind first over to open a new gound near Wakefield at the age of 72, **1949**.

R. C. Robertson-Glasgow (Somerset, 1920s)

IF I had my way, you wouldn't bat at all.

JOHN DANIELL, Somerset captain, in reply to Robertson-Glasgow asking his place in the batting order.

Emmott Robinson (Yorkshire)

ROBINSON seemed to be made out of the stuff of Yorkshire county. I imagine that the Lord one day gathered together a heap of Yorkshire clay and breathed into it and said, 'Emmott Robinson, go and bowl at the pavilion end for Yorkshire.'

NEVILLE CARDUS, *Good Days*. The amended version in Cardus's autobiography gives God a Yorkshire accent instead of Yorkshire clay.

Peter Roebuck (Somerset)

WATCHING Roebuck was like being at a requiem mass.

JIM LAKER after Roebuck scored 34, including two fours, in 2 hours 43 minutes *v* Surrey, **1985**. Roebuck had previously criticised Laker's 'dirge-like' commentating.

Peter Sainsbury (Hampshire)

I'M all right when his arm comes over but I'm out of form by the time the bloody ball gets here.

FRED TRUEMAN, describing his problems against Sainsbury, **1963**.

Arthur Shrewsbury (Nottinghamshire, England, 1880s)

JUST give me Arthur.

W. G. GRACE, asked to name his greatest contemporary batsman.

HE never seemed to make runs – they came.

G. L. JESSOP.

PUT me under the ground 22 yards from Arthur, so that I may send him a ball now and then.

ALFRED SHAW, asking to be buried near Shrewsbury, **1907**.

John Snow (Sussex, England)

HIS bowling performances and more especially his fielding have been so lacking in effort that the selection committee have no alternative.

SUSSEX SELECTORS, dropping England's pace bowler Snow, **1971**.

A really quick bowler when he wanted to be. . . . Snow had the typical fast bowler's moodiness, and he was a bit of a loner.

BOB WILLIS, *The Cricket Revolution*, **1981**.

Sir Gary Sobers (Notts, West Indies)

IT was not sheer slogging through strength, but scientific hitting with every movement working in harmony.

TONY LEWIS, Glamorgan's captain, on Gary Sobers' six sixes in an over for Notts at Swansea, **1968**.

F. R. Spofforth (Australia)

A tall, rather slim figure, but lissom, wiry, and full of vitality; a very high action and an atmosphere of undisguised hostility, and a subtle and unresting brain behind it all.

H. S. ALTHAM, *A History of Cricket*, **1926**.

HIS nickname, the Demon Bowler . . . appeared to be descriptive of his indefatigability at the critical moment of a match more than of his much rarer so-called 'lightning flashes'.

L. H. BACMEISTER, *The Cricketer*, **1928**.

David Steele (Northamptonshire, England)

A bank clerk going to war.

CLIVE TAYLOR, the *Sun*, as Steele defied West Indies pace bowlers, **1976**.

Micky Stewart (Surrey)

HE is representative of his time: an amateur type who became a professional.

PHIL PILLEY, *The Cricketer*.

MICKY's father . . . was, in fact, a London suburban bookmaker – and here, perhaps, is a hint of why Stewart has blended so easily into *professional* county cricket. He had become, so to speak, the amateur-type son of professional-type forbears.

PHIL PILLEY, *The Cricketer*.

Chris Tavaré (Kent, England)

WHEN he strolls away towards square leg . . . it is like an act of thanksgiving that the previous ball has been survived and a moment of prayer for the fibre to get through the next.

BOB WILLIS, *The Captain's Diary*, **1983**.

Freddie Trueman (Yorkshire, England)

WITHOUT rival, the ripest, the richest, the rip-roaringest individual performer on cricket's stage.

A. A. THOMSON, *The Cricketer*, **1961**.

FRED Trueman the mature fast bowler was a sharply pointed and astutely directed weapon; Fred Trueman the man has often been tactless, haphazard, crude, a creature of impulse. In Fred Trueman the public image, so many accretions of rumour and fiction have been deposited round the human core that the resultant figure is recognisable only to those who do not know him.

JOHN ARLOTT in *Fred*, **1971**.

FRED not only bowled fast. He was a fast bowler to the very depths of his soul.

JOHN HAMPSHIRE, *Family Argument*, **1983**.

I had asked my publishers to call my biography 'T'Definitive Volume on t'Finest Bloody Fast Bowler that Ever Drew Breath'. But the silly buggers just intend to call it 'Fred'.

FRED TRUEMAN, **1971**.

LOOK, Freddie, you've got lots of pitches in Yorkshire, but if you keep on treading so heavily, Lancashire won't even have one.

CHAIRMAN of the Old Trafford ground committee to Freddie Trueman during England v India Test match, **1952**.

TELL me, Fred, have you ever bowled a ball which merely went straight?

RICHARD HUTTON, in an exchange with Fred Trueman.

Victor Trumper (Australia)

VICTOR Trumper had the greatest charm and two strokes for every ball.

C. B. FRY, *Life Worth Living*, **1939**.

Glenn Turner (Worcestershire, New Zealand)

I know the reason he likes the one-day game. He thinks it's great because nobody gets the ball above stump-high. We wouldn't tolerate that attitude in Australia.

KIM HUGHES. Turner's reply was that Hughes, and fellow Australian David Hookes, 'are simply block-bash merchants'.

Derek Underwood (Kent, England)

I must have kept wicket, day in day out, to Derek Underwood for seven years now and I doubt if he's bowled ten full-tosses or long-hops in the whole of that time.

ALAN KNOTT, **1972**.

THE face of a choirboy, the demeanour of a civil servant and the ruthlessness of a rat catcher . . . Underwood is a mean pressure bowler who gives nothing away and expects nothing in return.

GEOFF BOYCOTT, *Opening Up*, **1980**.

IN the old days I was considered miserly, and I'd settle for bowling maiden after maiden. These days there are times when it's vital to get a wicket – and my team-mates expect it of me as the senior bowler – so I experiment more.

DEREK UNDERWOOD, **1985**.

Hedley Verity (Yorkshire, England)

HOSTILITY is not the same thing as say 'bodyline'. It marked Verity's bowling – he talked with his fingers – and he was a man who bowled as if in a mental abstraction, the batsman being the obstacle. He had that quality which never lets a batsman rest, never allows him an easy stroke, pinches him for foot space, makes him uneasy to step out in case he is stumped and haunts him with the feeling that he is going to be bowled round his legs by something he leaves alone.

WALTER HAMMOND.

Tom Walker (Hambledon, 1780s)

THE driest and most rigid-limbed chap I ever knew, his skin was like the rind of an old oak, and as sapless. I have seen his knuckles handsomely knocked about from Harris's bowling; but never saw any blood on his hands – you might just as well attempt to phlebotomize a mummy.

JOHN NYREN, *The Cricketers of My Time*.

Cyril Washbrook (Lancashire, England)

I have never felt so glad in my life as when I saw who was coming in.

PETER MAY on Washbrook's entrance in his comeback match after a five-year absence as England stood 17–3 *v* Australia at Headingley, **1956**.

Wasim Akram (Lancashire, Pakistan)

THREE years ago I said he was a better version of Hadlee and everyone laughed. But he is. He made me feel like some laborious blocker.

IMRAN KHAN, Pakistan captain, after Akram's 123 in a partnership of 191 with Imran against Australia, **1990**.

Everton Weekes and Frank Worrell (West Indies)

I considered Worrell the sounder in defence, Weekes the greater attacking force; Worrell the more graceful, Weekes the more devastating; Worrell the more effective on soft wickets, Weekes the more so on hard wickets. Worrell gives the bowler less to work on, Weekes has the wider range of strokes. Both are good starters but Weekes is the more businesslike; Worrell appeared to be enjoying an afternoon's sport; whereas Weekes was on the job six hours a day.

JEFFREY STOLLMEYER, former West Indian captain, on the two Bajan batsmen in *Everything under the Sun*, **1985**.

Bob Willis (Surrey, Warwickshire, England)

I don't go as far as that on my holidays.

FORMER TEST BOWLER on the length of Bob Willis's run-up.

BOWLER'S name?

CRY FROM EDGBASTON CROWD, **1985**. Willis had taken only nine Championship wickets the previous year.

Charles Wright (Nottinghamshire, England, 1890s)

WAS captain of Notts, and had also got a century in the University match. He was a most delightful person, but by no means the complete Encyclopaedia Britannica.

CYRIL FOLEY (Middlesex), *The Cricketer*, **1927**.

WELL, I never! Here's Chals come all the way from Nottin'am to 'ave a friendly game with us, and you go and do a thing like that to 'im.

W. G. GRACE to his brother E.M., who had successfully appealed for hitting the ball twice after W.G. had asked Wright to knock the ball back to him. According to Foley, W.G. was part of the plot.

Frank Woolley (Kent, England)

EASY to watch, difficult to bowl to, and impossible to write about. When you bowled to him there weren't enough fielders; when you wrote about him there weren't enough words.

R. C. ROBERTSON-GLASGOW, *Cricket Prints*, **1943**.

THE most graceful of the efficient, and the most efficient of the graceful.

I. A. R. PEEBLES, *Woolley – the Pride of Kent*, **1969**.

R. E. S. Wyatt (Warwickshire, Worcestershire, England)

I wasn't disputing your decision, Frank. I just couldn't believe that such an awful bowler could get me out twice.

FRANK WOOLLEY to umpire Frank Chester, when asked why he dallied at the crease after Wyatt dismissed him, Kent *v* Warwickshire at Dover, **1923**.

Teams

Hambledon, 1770/80s

No eleven in England could have had any chance with these men, and I think they might have beaten any twenty-two.

JOHN NYREN.

TROY has fallen and Thebes is a ruin. The pride of Athens is decayed, and Rome is crumbling to the dust. The philosophy of Bacon is wearing out, and the Victories of Marlborough have been overshadowed by greater laurels. All is vanity, but cricket; all is sinking in oblivion but you. Greatest of all elevens, fare ye well!

REV. JOHN MITFORD.

THEY were backbone players, ready to go till they dropped, and never sick or sorry in a match.

JOHN BOWYER of Surrey, The Players and England.

Gloucestershire, 1920s

ONLY two problems with our team. Brewers' droop and financial cramp. Apart from that we ain't bloody good enough.

CHARLIE PARKER, Gloucestershire and England slow bowler, quoted by David Foot in *Cricket's Unholy Trinity*, **1985**.

Somerset, 1920s

FOR many of us, who had the luck and the honour to play for Somerset, memory lingers on of a hard but humorous adventure.

R. C. ROBERTSON-GLASGOW, *The Cricketer*.

Yorkshire, 1930s

YORKSHIRE cricket is soulless. Bowl six good-length balls and they're all pushed safely back. Decide to toss one higher and slower and, crash, it goes for four. After that, the same remorseless push, push, push, until you make another mistake.

'TUBBY' OWEN-SMITH of Middlesex, **1937**, quoted by Bill Bowes in *Express Deliveries*, **1949**.

Kent, 1940s/50s

I'M not so sure that success can only be measured in terms of matches won. For those who like the social side of cricket, whether as player or spectator, Kent cricket is the answer. Hospitality is readily extended in the various tents around the ground.

ARTHUR PHEBEY, Kent opening batsman of the period.

Australia, 1955

I don't think we'll ever see a better fielding side. Eight of your team ran like stags and threw like bombs.

PETER MAY, England captain, **1955**.

Surrey, 1950s

THE spectator is fed up with seeing Laker and Lock, on helpful pitches, winning the County Championship for Surrey seven times in succession and making all international games in England a near farce.

W. E. BOWES, *The Cricketer*, **1959**.

THIS team plays cricket in the way that it should be played. There is no hint of that depressing feature, sometimes seen on county grounds, of obviously Tired Tims for whom a six-day week is business rather than pleasure.

TIMES EDITORIAL, August **1957**.

West Indies, 1963

[THEY] have shown us once again that cricket can and should be played with either obvious delight or communicable disappointment – a human game – which is a truth that lay long and deeply hidden in certain countries that should know better.

R. C. ROBERTSON-GLASGOW.

WE do not worry unduly about winning, losing or drawing. We wanted to impress the press and the public that our boys were pretty good cricketers and that they should come again much sooner than in eight years' time – and I think we have done that.

FRANK WORRELL at the end of the tour.

Sussex, 1963 (first Gillette Cup Winners)

THEY are an enterprising batting side, of course, but as I see it their attack is perfect for 1963 conditions. They possess five accurate seam bowlers who give nothing away, with spinners Bell and Oakman making contributions on rare occasions.

COLIN COWDREY, *The Cricketer*.

Derbyshire, 1960s

DERBYSHIRE batsmen always labour under certain difficulties both psychological and technical. They have no tradition to inherit, no heroes to emulate. They are regarded as subordinates, an inferior race with a secondary role; not much is expected of them and therefore not much is forthcoming. They know that 250 is enough in most games and therefore are incapable of aiming at higher totals. They bat just as well – or badly – on a bad wicket as a good one. Their aim is, by playing within their limitations, to scrape together enough runs to win matches.

GUY WILLATT, former Derbyshire player, **1970**.

Australia, 1970s/80s

THE Australians have different standards and ways of expressing themselves – and swearing has been part of their approach on the field.

GLENN TURNER, **1983**.

IT's going to be very hard to convince people back home that we really do have a lot of promising young players.

ALLAN BORDER after his **1985** side lost the Ashes.

Essex, 1970s/80s

THAT load of madmen will never win anything until they learn some self-discipline.

RAY ILLINGWORTH shortly before Essex won everything (quoted in Ray East, *A Funny Turn*, **1983**).

Pakistan, 1980s

THEY'VE always had a lot of talent, a lot of good players, but they're like eleven women. You know, they're all scratching each other's eyes out and wanting to do this and that. That has always been their downfall as a team.

IAN BOTHAM.

West Indies 1980s

IN their disregard of anybody being hit and hurt some West Indians appeared callous and reminded me of bully boys.

JACK FINGLETON on the West Indies' short-pitched bowling at The Oval, **1980**. (Taken from *Batting from Memory*, 1981.)

IN the field the most boring team I had seen, with their super-abundance of fast bowlers who bowled so many bouncers (and therefore unplayable balls), their slow over rates with their incomprehensibly long run-ups.

JACK FINGLETON, *Batting from Memory*.

I'VE been a professional for 18 years and what happened out there had nothing to do with cricket.

GEOFF HOWARTH, New Zealand batsman, reacting to the short-pitched methods of West Indian pace bowlers, Jamaica, **1985**.

CLIVE Lloyd's West Indians would have given Bradman's 1948 'unbeatables' a real run for their money. We'd have won, but only just.

NEIL HARVEY, **1980**.

IT is definitely worse than Bodyline, because there is no let-up, and it is just as fierce.

KEITH RIGG, former Australian player, on the West Indies' pace attack in Australia in **1988**.

THE West Indies pacemen have switched the attack to me to the body. It's not very pleasant.

ALLAN BORDER, Australian captain, **1988**.

WE don't breed brutal cricketers.

CLIVE LLOYD, West Indies manager, rejecting charges that West Indies played brutal cricket. **1988**.

IF every country had an attack like the West Indies, Test cricket would die pretty quickly. You can only think of survival, not playing shots.

ALLAN BORDER, Australian captain, after a fraught Melbourne Test, **1989**.

AT least we're bowling people out in less than a day, so that stuffs up this over-rate business.

CLIVE LLOYD, West Indies manager.

England, 1980s

ONE is always a little nervous when watching England bat.

PETER MAY, chairman of selectors, **1984**.

WE have not seen a match-winning performance from a bowler in Test cricket for far too long. We seem unable to bowl other sides out twice – hence we have not won many matches.

PETER MAY, still chairman of selectors, at the start of the **1988** season.

GETTING like Glamorgan, isn't it? When the weak link in the side is the only Welshman.

ANON COUNTY CRICKETER, on the number of South Africans playing for England.

IF I was bowling against this England team, I'd get a lot more Test wickets than I did; they're bloody scared.

CHARLIE GRIFFITH, former West Indian pace bowler, during England's tour of the Caribbean, **1981**.

HELL's teeth, I was a bloody greyhound next to this lot.

GEOFFREY BOYCOTT on England's pedestrian display *v* New Zealand, **1988**.

THE usual permutation of plebs: a few Gentlemen, some Professionals, a couple you'd rather not introduce to your mother – and at least one you'd cross Oxford Street to avoid.

FRANCES EDMONDS, *Daily Express*, **1985**.

CLOGGED! Now the bloomin' Dutch smash our shamed cricketers.

THE SUN after an England side's defeat in a one-day match in the Netherlands, **1989**.

2
Captains Courageous

A Captain's Lot

THERE'S only one captain of a side when I'm bowling – me.

SYDNEY BARNES.

WHY do so many players *want* to be captain?

DEREK UNDERWOOD, quoted by Mike Brearley in *The Art of Captaincy*, **1985**.

CRICKET teams have often suffered from captains who have arrived, done queer things, departed and been forgotten.

R. C. ROBERTSON-GLASGOW, *Cricket Prints*, **1943**.

THERE is very little wrong that a captain cannot attend to.

STUART SURRIDGE, Surrey captain, in letter about the state of the game to the *Sunday Times*, **1957**.

IT is a strange fact connected with cricket that a good captain is but seldom met with.

A. G. STEEL, *The Badminton Library – Cricket*, **1904**.

IT is easier for a football manager to 'play God', to read the riot act to the players, because he does not have to perform himself. Sales managers don't sell, foremen don't hump bricks. All cricket captains bat and field, and some bowl. We receive repeated intimations of our own fallibility.

MIKE BREARLEY, *The Art of Captaincy*, **1985**.

A public relations officer, agricultural consultant, psychiatrist, accountant, nursemaid and diplomat.

D. J. INSOLE's definition of a captain's duties.

I find I am playing every ball, bowling every ball and fielding every ball. The captaincy has cost me over six hundred runs a season. I am snapping at my wife and children and sleeping no more than four hours a night.

MICKY STEWART, **1971**, the year Surrey won the Championship.

As a county captain, one seems to spend an inordinate amount of time filling in forms of which no one takes the slightest notice.

RAY ILLINGWORTH, *Yorkshire and Back*, **1980**.

YOU'RE in charge from the moment you wake up until you buy a pint in the bar for the other players after the game. At times there are so many demands before play starts that I suddenly realise I've had no time for a knock-up myself.

M. C. J. NICHOLAS on his first season as captain of Hampshire, **1985**.

YOU are carrying all the prejudices of England. You are representing deep and paranoid urges, jingoistic sentiments you may prefer to distance yourself from. But it is unavoidable.

MIKE BREARLEY, to Simon Barnes of *The Times*, **1987**.

THE player who stands at fine leg and occasionally refrains from admiring the female talent just long enough to castigate his captain for not changing the bowling is not recognisable as the same man when the onus of decisive action falls on him.

D. J. INSOLE.

CAPTAINCY seems to involve half-hearing conversations which you'd rather not hear at all.

PETER ROEBUCK, Somerset batsman, in *It Never Rains*, **1984**.

SOME skippers seem to be living in cloud-cuckoo land when they set their targets. I never cease to be amazed when a captain of a side that struggled to average two runs an over suddenly asks opponents to make in the region of eight runs an over to win.

RAY ILLLINGWORTH, *Captaincy*, **1980**.

WHEN I win the toss on a good pitch, I bat. When I win the toss on a doubtful pitch, I think about it a bit and then I bat. When I win the toss on a very bad pitch, I think about it a bit longer, and then I bat.

W. G. GRACE.

I suppose he got it for winning the toss.

BOB WILLIS, losing Warwickshire captain, after Lancashire's John Abrahams, who scored nought and did not bowl, won Man of the Match award in Benson and Hedges Cup Final, **1984**.

'A dynamic bowling change' you write about is probably sheer luck nine times out of ten. OK, you bring on someone and he gets a wicket – great, but I haven't solved the mystery of the universe, have I?

GRAHAM GOOCH, **1988**.

My conscience is clear, Yorkshire had no chance of winning and my job was to prevent the other side from winning.

BRIAN CLOSE, after time-wasting allegations which lost him the England captaincy, Warwickshire *v* Yorkshire at Edgbaston, **1967**.

I felt as if I had come third in an egg and spoon race at school and been awarded the prize because the first two had been disqualified.

COLIN COWDREY, assuming captaincy from Brian Close after time-wasting controversy, **1967**.

WHAT do they expect me to do? Walk round in a T-shirt with 'I'm in Charge' on it?

DAVID GOWER, responding to the selectors' vocal doubts about his restrained style of captaincy, **1986**.

I'M in Charge.

LOGO on T-shirt handed down by David Gower to his successor as England captain, Mike Gatting, **1986**. Gower had one printed after all.

THE T-shirt was perhaps a mistake. But I couldn't resist it. Captaincy means more than vigorous arm-waving.

DAVID GOWER, later that year.

IT was thought apparently that the missing 10 per cent, the difference between finishing second and first in the Sunday League for example, could be achieved with a change of captaincy.

DAVID GRAVENEY on losing the Gloucestershire captaincy in **1988**.

ENGLAND seem to have a fixation with so-called leadership qualities – and it usually means background.

GEOFFREY BOYCOTT, **1981**.

A 'keeper should be captain only on the rarest of occasions in first-class cricket. The mental strains of keeping wicket are just too much to be able to spend the time worrying about the nuts and bolts. The captain should be detached and analytical while it is the 'keeper's job to bawl out fielders and slap bowlers on the backside, telling them they're bowling well.

BOB TAYLOR in *Standing Up, Standing Back*, **1985**.

GOODNESS knows what Simmons's thoughts were as he shared twelfth man duties with Clive Lloyd, unusual roles, incidentally, for a county's vice-captain and captain.

RICHARD STREETON, *The Times*, **1986**. Lloyd and Simmons had not been selected against Leicestershire in the first home match of the season.

THEY can all resign themselves to the fact that none of them will ever be quite as good as the talkative gentleman with the packet of ham sandwiches who sits square with the wicket on every county ground in the land.

D. J. INSOLE, on the fate awaiting the eight new county captains, **1963**.

Leaders of Men

G. O. (Gubby) Allen and D. R. Jardine (England)

ALLOWING for the relative skill of both sides, Allen got more out of his team than did Douglas Jardine. Allen was a keen student, so was Jardine, but where Jardine belonged to the atomic bomb era, Gubby fought his battles with pike and spears. When Gubby's battle ended, the noise and strife ended with it, but in the tough Scot's case, the 'death dust' lingered for a considerable time.

ARTHUR MAILEY.

Warwick Armstrong (Australia)

OFTEN on a warm June afternoon on the mellow county grounds of England Warwick would doze at point and allow the game to drift like a ship left in the hands of its crew. There were very few batsmen in England in 1921 who could back-cut, and Warwick, after having a couple of glasses of ale at lunch, knew that there was a sanctuary in one part of the field where his siesta had little chance of being interrupted.

ARTHUR MAILEY.

Kim Barnett (Derbyshire)

EVERY time I champion Kim's cause at Lord's I am asked 'Is he a gentleman?' and I reply, 'One of nature's!' Yet they keep asking the same question.

GUY WILLATT, Derbyshire cricket committee chairman, on Barnett's failure to be tried as one of the five England captains in **1988**.

I'VE played under Clive Lloyd, one of the all-time great captains, and I could only say that Kim is the best I have come across apart from Clive. If he adopted the attitude of so many other professional players, thinking only of himself, he would have got 1800 runs a season. But he plays for his team.

MICHAEL HOLDING, Derbyshire's West Indian fast bowler, **1988**.

Ian Botham (Somerset, England)

HE captains the side like a great big baby.

HENRY BLOFELD, journalist, on Botham's leadership of England in West Indies, **1981**.

HE always gets the benefit of my help. I haven't known him bothering asking much, have you?

GEOFFREY BOYCOTT, prior to West Indies tour, **1981**.

To appoint him to that position again would be to run the risk of reducing the greatest English cricketer since W. G. Grace from genius to mediocrity.

MIKE BREARLEY, on possibility of Botham returning to England captaincy, in *Phoenix from the Ashes*, **1982**.

Allan Border (Australia)

A terrier, who barks and growls and will not give in. In trouble, Border spits and scraps [but] hides his passion. Border inspires best those as regular and capable as himself.

PETER ROEBUCK, **1989**.

Geoffrey Boycott (Yorkshire, England)

YOU cannot motivate a team with the word 'I'. Geoff cannot fool anyone; they know he's totally, almost insanely, selfish.

IAN BOTHAM in *It Sort of Clicks*, Botham and Peter Roebuck, **1986**.

HE is so dedicated to the perfection and exploitation of his own batting technique that he is sometimes oblivious to the feelings and aspirations of his team-mates.

ARTHUR CONNELL, chairman of Yorkshire committee which replaced Boycott as captain, **1978**.

EVEN the Yorkshire Ripper got a fair trial, but I've never been given a single chance.

GEOFFREY BOYCOTT on being overlooked as England cricket captain.

Sir Donald Bradman (Australia)

THE Don, it appears, had two views of bouncers – one when they were bowled against him and the other when bowled by his side with no fear of retaliation.

JACK FINGLETON on Bradman's failure to dissuade Lindwall and Miller from excessive use of bouncers, **1946**. (Taken from *Batting from Memory*.)

As a skipper he was merciless, determined from the outset in 1948 to get a record which meant as much as any to him – that of leading an unbeaten Australian team in England.

JACK FINGLETON, *Batting from Memory*, **1981**.

APART from [one instance] I never heard him praise a player unduly, or motivate his team with discussions of tactics. Perhaps his main resource as a leader was the example he set his men in concentration and the relentlessness of his attack.

JACK FINGLETON, *Batting from Memory*, **1981**.

I didn't get on with him as a man. We had nothing in common. But as a batsman, captain and tactician, he had no equal.

KEITH MILLER.

Mike Brearley (Middlesex, England)

IN Mike Brearley's unarrogant flat, where he lives alone – rumpled bedclothes in mid-afternoon and unwashed plates on the kitchen table – I made a beeline for the bookshelves. I spotted *Games People Play*, *The Divided Self*, *Human Aggression*, *The Art of Loving*, *Perspectives in Group Therapy*, *The Miracle Worker*, *The Poems of Auden*. I wonder what books Greig and Boycott have on their shelves?

DAVID BENEDICTUS.

He's got a degree in people, hasn't he?

RODNEY HOGG, Australian fast bowler.

On Friday I watched J. M. Brearley directing his fieldsmen very carefully. He then looked up at the sun and made a gesture which suggested that it should move a little squarer. Who is this man?

LETTER to the *Guardian*, **1981**.

The statistics suggest that he is one of the great England captains. The luckiest would be nearer the truth.

RAY ILLINGWORTH on Brearley's first spell as England captain, **1980**.

That man must be a bigger ass than I thought he was.

CLIVE LLOYD replying to Brearley's criticisms of him as captain.

F. R. Brown (Northamptonshire, England)

F. R. BROWN was of that type of Englishman not always finding favour in the dominions.

W. E. BOWES on Brown's management of the England team in Australia, **1958/9**, in *The Cricketer Spring Annual 1959*.

Ian Chappell (Australia)

Playing against a team with Ian Chappell as captain turns a cricket match into gang warfare.

MIKE BREARLEY, lecture at St John's College, Cambridge, **1980**.

Brian Close (Yorkshire, Somerset, England)

Eh, up, Raymond, t'rudder's gone again.

JIMMY BINKS, Yorkshire wicket-keeper, to Ray Illingworth on Close's tendency to let his mind wander.

THERE were times when Closey could make Walter Mitty appear a modest realist.

RAY EAST, from *A Funny Turn*, **1983**.

Colin Cowdrey (Kent, England)

HE could never make up his mind whether to call heads or tails.

RAY ILLINGWORTH.

IN view of the settled weather and the Manchester holidays next week, Mr Cowdrey will not necessarily enforce the follow-on if this situation arises.

G. HOWARD, Lancashire secretary, during Colin Cowdrey's first Test as England captain *v* India, **1959**.

Ted Dexter (Sussex, England)

THERE is no doubt that Dexter can handle a bat, but who is going to handle Dexter?

ENGLAND SELECTOR after appointment of Dexter as captain, **1962**.

CHARISMA is not the same as leadership . . . Dexter's main failure was that he easily became bored . . . he was an excellent theorist, but when his theories failed to work or when he had no particular bright ideas he would drift and the whole team drifted with him. I would guess that Dexter, in those days, was more interested in ideas than people.

MIKE BREARLEY, *The Art of Captaincy*, **1985**.

J. W. H. T. Douglas (Essex, England)

HE has many assets as a captain . . . but he cannot be called a great tactician as he occasionally takes time to see the obvious.

PORTRAIT OF DOUGLAS in *The Cricketer* on his appointment to captain England *v* Australia, **1921**.

WELL, if you're going to bowl with the new one, you can bloody well go on with the old one, too.

SYDNEY BARNES to Douglas, after he chose to take the new ball himself, MCC in Australia, **1911/12**.

JOHNNY used to bowl them in, then chuck the ball to me to bowl them out.

CECIL PARKIN, denied new ball by Douglas, on MCC tour of Australia, **1920/21**.

Keith Fletcher (Essex, England)

THAT frail appearance is deceptive, a cloak disguising a strong will. The pottering gait and shuffling feet, the tangled pads and the quizzical air create an impression of a quiet, mystical leader, a Napoleon of cricket. It is all nonsense! Fletcher is far from meek, he is a thoroughly professional, fighting captain. He asks nothing and gives less.

PETER ROEBUCK, *Slices of Cricket*, **1982**.

HE is not a man easily deflected from his purpose. His team has succeeded because, eventually, it adopted the characteristics of its captain – an unforgiving, shrewd and persevering approach to a hard game.

PETER ROEBUCK, the *Guardian*, **1984**.

Mike Gatting (Middlesex, England)

WHAT worries me is his tolerance level.

JOHN WOODCOCK, *The Times*, on appointment of Gatting as England captain, **1986**.

HE is an artisan skipper, a welder of personalities, who by his own example will get his men to play for him. He will not ask them to do what he himself would not.

MIKE SELVEY, **1988**.

YET whatever the good points he is only as strong as his weakest link. So uncomplicated is he, so honest, that he cannot hide his feelings. And, however much he and his team were wronged by umpires initially, and later by his board, his own dam of self-discipline . . . has been irreparably and publicly breached.

MIKE SELVEY, **1988**.

THERE have been, too, the worrying tactical decisions for which, whether or not they have been made by committee, the captain carries the can . . . a lingering reticence about his spinners that still discourages him from attacking with them, and the apparent advice to his pacemen in Karachi that they should persist with short bowling even when their instincts told them otherwise.

MIKE SELVEY, **1988**.

PASSENGERS are reminded that they should be as quiet as possible during this trip because Mike Gatting is trying to catch up on his sleep.

AIR HOSTESS on the Melbourne to Adelaide flight. Gatting, the new England captain, had arrived late for play in the Melbourne Test after oversleeping, **1986**.

Graham Gooch (Essex, England)

As much charisma as a wet fish.

TED DEXTER, shortly before he became chairman of the England committee that, by the end of the year, had elected Gooch captain, **1989**.

David Gower (Leicestershire, England)

REAL officer class. Languid self-possession. Confront him with a firing squad and he'd decline the blindfold.

PAT POCOCK, after Gower was appointed captain of England, **1989**.

HE is too laid-back, perhaps too self-centred. Gower lacks the authority to impose his will when senior players are questioning his tactics. And he cannot whip his men into renewed effort when their spirits are flagging. That was only too evident when England were in the West Indies in 1986. They just gave up. They thought: 'Our opponents are better than we are and if we lose it's no big deal.' No real captain would have allowed his team to surrender meekly like that. Gower did.

CLIVE LLOYD, **1988**.

IT is quite funny watching him. From being a person who disregarded discipline – he wasn't a rebel, he just ignored it – he has been put in a situation where he has to determine the framework. And that is why we have called him TC (Turn Coat), because he has talked of compulsory nets.

GRAEME FOWLER in *Fox on the Run*, **1988**, on Gower's leadership in India.

W. G. Grace (Gloucestershire, England)

THERE was an unwritten law prevailing in those days – a rule, I believe, confined to those under 'W.G.'s' leadership – which forbade any person or persons airing opinions on the game unless he or they had scored a century in first-class cricket. As in the majority of matches there was only one man on the side who had achieved the feat, we were not greatly troubled by listening to immature thoughts.

G. L. JESSOP on Gloucestershire under Grace.

Tony Greig (Sussex, England)

HE was the first England player I remember actively indulging in gamesmanship.

BOB TAYLOR, **1985**.

THERE's only one head bigger than Greig's – and that's Birkenhead.

FRED TRUEMAN.

IF Greig fell off the Empire State Building, he'd land on a furniture van fitted with mattresses.

ENGLAND COLLEAGUE, **1976**.

WHAT has to be remembered of course is that he is not an Englishman by birth or upbringing, but only by adoption. It is not the same thing as being English through and through.

JOHN WOODCOCK, *The Times* cricket correspondent, on Greig's defection to Packer when England captain.

I have no respect for him as a cricketer or as a man.

IAN CHAPPELL, **1979**.

Sir Len Hutton (Yorkshire, England)

THE outstanding characteristic of his captaincy was shrewdness. He made no romantic gestures; he lit no fires of inspiration. He invited admiration rather than affection and would have exchanged both for effective obedience. A Test match rubber played under Hutton's captaincy became a business undertaking with its principal satisfactions represented by the dividends paid. Hutton did not expect his players to enjoy their Test matches until the scoreboard showed victory. He could not countenance a light-hearted approach to any cricket match when the result of that match had a meaning. He wanted his team-mates to be untiringly purposeful.

J. M. KILBURN, *Yorkshire Post* correspondent, on Hutton's retirement, in *The Cricketer*, **1956**.

Ray Illingworth (Yorkshire, Leicestershire, England)

THE severest criticism of Ray Illingworth is that he did not sufficiently discourage the element of selfishness which is part of most professional cricketers.

MIKE BREARLEY, **1973**.

D. R. Jardine (Surrey, England)

A dour remorseless Scot, 130 years after his time. He should have gone to Australia in charge of a convict hulk.

JACK FINGLETON, Australian opening bat.

HE is a queer fellow. When he sees a cricket ground with an Australian on it, he goes mad.

SIR PELHAM WARNER, letter to Governor of South Australia, **1934**, after the Bodyline rumpus.

HE can be a powerful friend but a relentless enemy. He gives no quarter and asks none. He is a fighter, every inch of him. He will see a job through, no matter what the consequences, and will never admit defeat.

BILL BOWES, *Express Deliveries*, **1949**.

Clive Lloyd (Lancashire, West Indies)

THIS was not great captaincy, it was barbarism.

SUNIL GAVASKAR, on Lloyd's handling of the West Indian pace attack, **1976**.

HE doesn't work by changing the structure of things, he works by changing the people in the structure. He tries to mould them, get them round to his way of thinking and put them on the right track. He believes that the best way of having a good ship is to mould the crew, not to change the shipping company. I don't always agree. Clive is one of the most powerful people in cricket, yet he doesn't overtly use his influence. He always wants to do things quietly, and it just doesn't work – at least not with Lancashire.

GRAEME FOWLER in *Fox on the Run*, **1988**.

WITHOUT being unkind, a donkey could lead West Indies at the moment. But put Clive Lloyd in charge of Australia and even he'd struggle.

KEITH FLETCHER, reacting to Hughes' resignation of Australian captaincy, **1984**.

A. C. MacLaren (Lancashire, England)

A pessimistic commander, I have heard old timers say he was liable to enter the dressing-room clutching his head and saying 'Look what they've given me this time,' or 'Gracious me! Don't tell me you're playing!' which cannot have been very good for morale.

IAN PEEBLES.

ENGLAND may have had worse captains, but I would be hard put to it to name two or three.

ALAN GIBSON, *The Times*, on the centenary of MacLaren's birth, **1971**.

SORRY sir!
Don't be sorry, Barnes, you're coming to Australia with me!

EXCHANGE between Sydney Barnes and A. C. MacLaren after MacLaren had been struck on the hand in the Old Trafford nets in **1901**. MacLaren was England captain, Barnes a Lancashire League professional. Barnes made the trip.

P. B. H. May (Surrey, England)

EVERYONE knows, after Australia, that May is no squealer, no matter how provoked.

ROBIN MARLAR on the controversial **1959/60** 'chucking' tour.

Keith Miller (Australia)

ONE of you bugger off, and the rest scatter.

KEITH MILLER, captaining New South Wales, when told he had 12 players on the field.

Viv Richards (West Indies)

HAUGHTY and proud, but volatile too, a man capable of rages. In trouble Richards blazes or broods, wears his passion on his sleeve. He is easiest on his equals, or on youngsters in awe of him.

PETER ROEBUCK, **1989**.

BEFORE the start of the match he dismissed the idea of West Indian vulnerability to spin. When things went wrong his manner changed to that of a man who thought his team was being nobbled. It was hard to tell if he was being cool or uninterested on the field. Maybe he wanted to express contempt for this sort of cricket. Occasionally the umpires felt the lash of his tongue. Mostly the game simply drifted on.

PETER ROEBUCK on Richards' captaincy as Border took seven for 46 and Australia took a lead of 177 on a spinner's pitch, Fourth Test in Sydney, **1989**.

M. J. K. Smith (Warwickshire, England)

HIS approach to a problem was to sit in a chair with the *Daily Telegraph* crossword, doze off, wake up, finish the crossword and then fire some broadsides.

COLIN COWDREY in *MCC*, **1976**.

Bob Willis (Surrey, Warwickshire, England)

ENGLAND have at least nine captains out there. Unfortunately Bob Willis is not one of them.

HENRY BLOFELD, during late stages of England's three-run win over Australia in Melbourne Test, **1982–3** tour.

BOB always led from the standpoint that if he put in 100 per cent effort, and if he bowled to his full potential and we fielded and batted to our full potential, we would beat any side in the world. Tactics ended at that. It was 'Follow me, men!'

GRAEME FOWLER, *Fox on the Run*, **1988**.

IT was always safety first. He has got his own ideas, his own beliefs, and he is rigid.

GRAEME FOWLER, as above.

I am a born pessimist.

BOB WILLIS, *The Captain's Diary*, **1983**.

Norman Yardley (Yorkshire, England)

A kinder or more considerate captain never walked on to a field.

SIR LEN HUTTON, *50 Years in Cricket*, **1984**.

3

The Game that Was

Cricket Through the Ages

As a scholler in the free school of Guildeford he and several of his fellowes did run and play there at cricket and other plaies.

JOHN DERRICK, gent, testimony during reign of Henry VIII, **1549**.

I present Ralph West, Edmund Hartley, Richard Slaughter, William Martin, Richard Martin Junior, together with others whose names I have no notice of, for playing at Cricket in the Churchyard on Sunday, the fifthe of Maye, after sufficient warning had been given to the contrarie, for three special reasons: first, for it is contrarie to the 7th Article; second, that they are used to break the Church windows with their balls; and thirdly, for that little children had like to have their braynes beaten out with the cricket batt.

INDICTMENT of the above at Chichester Assizes by a Churchwarden from Boxgrove Deanery, **1622**.

Two Londoners striving for expedition to gain the ball, met each other with such fierceness, that, hitting their heads together, they both fell backwards without stirring hand or foot, and lay deprived of sense for a considerable time, and 'tis not yet known whether they will recover.

REPORT on London *v* Kent at Islington, **1720**, in *The Postman*. London won.

YE pitching of ye first Wicket is to be determined by ye cast of a piece of Money.

FIRST code of rules, Law I, **1744**.

IF ye Wicket is Bowled down, its Out.

FIRST CODE OF RULES, **1744**: Laws for Ye Strikers.

WHEN ye Ball has been in hand by one of ye Keepers or Stopers, and ye Player has been at home, He may go where he pleases till ye next ball is bowled.

FIRST CODE OF RULES, **1744**.

LORDS and gentleman, clergymen and lawyers . . . associate themselves with butchers and cobblers in such diversions.

THE BRITISH CHAMPION, **1743**, criticising cricket matches.

[THESE matches] draw numbers of people from their employment to the ruin of their families. It brings together crowds of apprentices and servants whose time is not their own. It propagates a spirit of idleness at a juncture when, with the utmost industry, our debts, taxes, and decay of trade will scarce allow us to get bread.

THE BRITISH CHAMPION, **1743**.

IT [cricket] is a most notorious and shameless breach of the laws, as it gives the most open encouragement to gambling.

THE BRITISH CHAMPION, **1743**.

NUMBERS of my friends have intimated that the taking of Six-pence admittance has been very prejudicial to me; these [notices] are to inform them that for the future they shall be admitted for Two-pence, and the favour of their Company greatly acknowledged by Their very humble servant, George Smith.

NOTICE posted by the owner of the HAC ground, George Smith, after an increase in admission from 2d to 6d had caused a fall in gates from around 7000 to 200, **1744**.

CRICKET is, to be sure, a manly game and not bad in itself, but it is the ill-use made of it, by betting above £10 upon it, that is bad and against the laws.

JUDGE'S comment during a lawsuit over a betting debt, **1748**.

I could tell you of Lord Montfort's making cricket matches and fetching up parsons by express from different parts of England to play on Richmond Green.

HORACE WALPOLE, **1749**.

A young fellow, a butcher, being entrusted with about £40 by his mistress to buy cattle in Smithfield Market, instead went into the Artillery Ground and sported away the whole sum in betting on the cricket players.

ST JAMES'S CHRONICLE, **1765**.

A wet day, only three members present, nine bottles of wine.

EXTRACT from early minutes of Hambledon Club.

HALF the county would be present, and all their hearts with us. Little Hambledon pitted against All England was a proud thought for the Hampshire men. Defeat was glory in such a struggle – Victory, indeed, made us only a 'little lower than angels'.

JOHN NYREN on cricket at Hambledon, **1780s**.

MANY [attend] out of compliment to Sir Horace . . . and, as he gives a very magnificent ball and supper on Friday, it would not be so polite to attend that without paying a compliment to his favourite amusement.

LETTER from Lady Hales to Mrs Phillips (Susan Burney) explaining why Hampshire society turned up *en masse* for Sir Horace Mann's match *v* Duke of Dorset, **1782**.

WE are happy to hear that the report of Mr Louch's being killed at Bourne Paddock by a ball from the point of the bat, struck with such force that it lodged in his body, is devoid of foundation. Yet the melancholy tale occasioned some debates in the club whether the striker was fairly out.

REPORT of the injury to George Louch (Kent) in a match *v* Hampshire, **1789**. It was widely believed including by his team-mates that Louch had been killed.

Deth minds a krikketer no more
Than he does cracking nuts.
Louch could not stop the ball before
He cocht hur in his Guts.

EPITAPH on Louch's 'demise' by a Kent colleague.

DESCENDING to the office of a coachman and driving his own carriage is not altogether compatible with a high rank and station, the more so when it is done in a public manner. The making of his own lamplighter a partner at a game of cricket is equally censurable.

THE TIMES, **1788**, on the behaviour of a Brighton gentleman.

ALTHOUGH we have all on occasions enjoined proper muscular exercise, yet we strongly reprobate that of cricket, which is in all respects too violent, and, from the positions into which players must necessarily throw themselves, cannot fail to be productive of frequent injury to the body. Indeed, we have witnessed several melancholy accidents which lately happened in our neighbourhood; from the awkward posture occasioned by employing both arms at the same time in striking a distant object.

DR WILLICH'S DOMESTIC ENCYCLOPAEDIA, **1802**.

Too poor to purchase a monument to this good man, his parishioners erected his wooden leg upon his grave. In that fertile clime, it miraculously took root and for many years provided a bountiful harvest of bats.

CARR'S DICTIONARY OF EXTRAORDINARY ENGLISH CRICKETERS on Reverend Elisha Fawcett, c. **1817**.

CRICKET is unalloyed by love of lucre and mean jealousies . . . the approbation and applause of the spectators being the sole reward.

LORD FREDERICK BEAUCLERK, speech to Thatched House Tavern, **1838**.

THE Kent people thought we had sold the match which, of course, was nonsense; but Alfred Mynn was hissed in Maidstone Market.

SIR EMILIUS BAYLEY on Kent's defeat by All England by nine wickets after scoring 278 in their first innings at Canterbury, **1840**.

CRICKET grounds be laid out at each end of the barrack stations throughout the United Kingdom for the use of officers and privates.

DUKE OF WELLINGTON, Commander in Chief, order, **1841**.

I went out into the country, and had the pleasure of seeing a match of cricket, in which a noble earl, the Lord Lieutenant of his county, was playing with the tradesmen, the labourers and all around him, and I believe that he lost no respect from that course – they loved him better, but they did not respect him less. I believe that if they themselves associated more with the lower classes of society, the kingdom of England would be in a far safer, and society in a far sounder, condition.

BARON ALDERSON, addressing grand jury of Suffolk, **1844**.

IF the present system of bowling is continued, we would strongly advise that suits of armour from the Tower of London be forwarded to all members at Lord's.

LORD WILLIAM PITT-LENNOX, **1860**, four years before MCC legalised overarm bowling.

WELL, I'm damned! They aren't black after all. If I'd knowed, I wunna come.

REACTION of a spectator on arrival of Australian tourists by train to Nottingham, **1878**.

CAPTAINS and secretaries of hundreds of weak clubs would find the difficulties of getting the eleven to the ground with punctuality to be vastly increased if the team knew beforehand that 'the other fellows' were going to bat first.

CHARLES PARDON, editor of *Wisden*, on advantages of tossing for innings, **1890**.

A cricketer's visit to Cambridge in the old President's days was never complete without an attack of the presidential 'Bollinger'.

A. G. STEEL, *Wisden*, **1890**.

OF all inventions that ever worked a revolution in cricket, nothing had more effect than the heavy roller and the mowing machine. The old scythe, however deftly wielded, left a tuft of grass here and there.

HON. R. H. LYTTELTON, *Wisden*, **1892**.

THEIR [boundaries] gradual introduction, dating from the [18]60s, had an adverse effect on deep fielding, and especially on throwing, to which the simultaneous urbanisation of the country also contributed.

H. S. ALTHAM, *A History of English Cricket*, **1926**.

IT was a serious thing not to stop a hard hit when the ball had to be followed until it was overtaken, and many balls used to be stopped which are now allowed to pass by as 'it is only 4'.

R. A. H. MITCHELL in W. A. Bettesworth's *Chats on the Cricket Field*, **1892**.

EVEN when a man is in most perfect condition he is a little pumped when he has run a fiver or a sixer, and numberless wickets have been lost because a man was too pumped to be able to play the next ball with confidence after a big hit.

V. E. WALKER in W. A. Bettesworth's *Chats on the Cricket Field*, **1892**.

THE practice of leaving balls to the off alone is downright bad cricket. If the ball is off the wicket it ought to be hit somehow or other.

AN OLD CAMBRIDGE CAPTAIN, *Wisden*, **1895**.

MEN stand in the field today like so many 'little mounds of earth' . . . the energy, the life, the ever-watchfulness of 10 years ago are gone, and in their place are lethargy, laziness and a wonderful yearning for rest.

D. L. A. JEPHSON, Surrey captain and lob bowler, *Wisden*, **1901**.

'Mr Jones, does it matter what I do?'
'No, Alletson, I don't think it matters what you do.'
'Oh, then I'm not half going to give Tom Killick some stick.'

EXCHANGE between the Notts captain Arthur Jones and Edwin Alletson before Alletson went out to bat *v* Sussex at Hove in 1911, with Notts facing apparently certain defeat. Alletson hit 189 in 90 minutes. (Quoted in Benny Green, *A History of Cricket*.)

AUDUN struck the ball over Grettir's head, so that he could not reach it. Grettir . . . fetched the ball, brought it back, and, going up to Audun, drove it straight into his forehead, so that the skin was broken. Audun then struck at Grettir with the bat he was holding.

SAGA OF GRETTIR THE STRONG (1010), cited in letter to *The Cricketer*, **1927**.

THE Midfjord cricket week of 1010 is, indeed, a strange thought. Iceland had been colonised from Norway rather more than 100 years before, and at about the same period when other Norsemen and Danes were making their own all that part of England north of a line from Chester to London. Can it be to them that we owe the game, as we owe so much else? Can Yorkshire trace her prowess to the fact that she is the most purely Norse of all English counties?

LETTER to *The Cricketer*, **1927**.

THIS modern scoffing at tradition is a product of super-democracy. Tradition is a hell of a good thing. It's what takes a regiment through hell.

PELHAM WARNER, **1933**.

W. G. GRACE was a Victorian but the game he transformed into a national institution was not Victorian either in origin or essence. It was a creation of pre-Victorian England . . . the England of the early Dickens and of William Hazlitt. It was an England still unconquered by the Industrial Revolution. It travelled by saddle and carriage. Whenever it could, it ate and drank prodigiously. It was not finicky in morals. It enjoyed life. . . . There were rulers and rules, the educated and the uneducated.

C. L. R. JAMES, Marxist historian, in *Beyond a Boundary*, **1963**.

4
The Noble Arts

Batting, Bowling, Fielding

WHEN you're both a batter and a bowler you enjoy yourself twice as much.

GEORGE HIRST.

HAVING seen the new scoreboard at Lord's, I notice that batsmen, and indeed fielders, are given both their surnames and initials. The bowlers, however, merit only their surnames. Is this a sign of the times?

OLIVER GRAVELL, letter to *The Times*, **1988**.

BATTING is a major trial before an eleven-man jury.

RICHIE BENAUD.

HE who strikes the ball with loving care is a gentleman. He who strokes it with hawk eyes is a worried man. He who blocks fast bowlers and belts spinners is a wise man.

PETER ROEBUCK, *Slices of Cricket*, **1982**.

I should like to say that good batsmen are born, not made; but my long experience comes up before me, and tells me that it is not so.

W. G. GRACE, *Cricket*, **1891**.

FIND out where the ball is. Go there. Hit it.

RANJI's three precepts of batsmanship.

THA knows one thing I learned about cricket: tha can't put in what God left out. Tha sees two kinds of cricketers, them that uses a bat as if they are shovelling muck and them that plays proper and like as not God showed both of 'em how to play.

WILFRED RHODES, from Michael Parkinson's *Cricket Mad*, **1969**.

ANY fool can play forward.

A. C. MACLAREN, *The Cricketer*, **1921**.

THEY were nearly all made off the back foot.

JACK HOBBS, explaining why the 85 county centuries he made after the First World War did not match those gathered in his youth. (Source: *Wisden* obituary, **1964**.)

THEY must learn to play off the back foot, because that is the only solution against fast bowling.

DENIS COMPTON on England's batting problems against West Indies, 10 July **1988**.

I would like to see our players getting more on to the front foot, thrusting the left pad down the pitch. It is usually fatal to try to play these West Indians off the back foot.

SIR LEN HUTTON, 24 July **1988**.

THERE is probably a greater premium on temperament for a batsman than for any player in any branch of sport.

SIR DONALD BRADMAN, *The Art of Cricket*, **1958**.

NERVES play as important a part in batsmanship as skill.

G. L. JESSOP.

DON'T give advice to a batsman going in: if he's inexperienced, it will only make him nervous; if he is an old hand, it is generally unnecessary. Give him credit and opportunity to use his own judgement; if he doesn't do so at first, he soon will.

GILBERT JESSOP, in Foreword to James Thorpe's *Cricket Bag*, **1929**.

To stand ideally is either to inflict upon yourself a form of astigmatism or of painful neck wrenching.

A. E. KNIGHT, *The Complete Cricketer*, **1906**.

IF he [the batsman] uses the 'one-eyed' stance, it is a case for variation of pace. The reason . . . is that the bridge of his nose now intercepts the sight of his right eye and he is really looking at the ball only with one eye, which means the ball during its flight seems nearer to him than it is; the ball only gets into the proper focus at a point well on its journey.

F. R. SPOFFORTH in G. W. Beldham and C. B. Fry's *Great Bowlers*, **1906**.

I could never read the scores on the board . . . the specialist said to me: 'Who leads you out to bat?'

NEIL HARVEY, Australian batsman, admitting defective eyesight.

YOU don't need footwork in batting, just hands and eye.

MAJID KHAN to Glamorgan team-mates, **1969**.

I hear a lot about this wonderful footwork, but they never seem to go forward – they're always crawling backwards.

LIONEL PALAIRET on the England batsmen's difficulties with Warwick Armstrong, **1920/21**.

STANDING with your bat in the air destroys rhythm and balance. Our batters stand much easier at the crease. Our bats are also very much lighter than the Englishmen's, and they are getting lighter all the time.

BOBBY SIMPSON, Australian manager, as the inquest into England's batting failures intensified in **1989**.

WHEN you are in all day the bat never feels heavy. It is only when you are in and out quickly that it weighs.

COLIN COWDREY in *MCC*, **1976**.

WHEN I'm coming, I say 'Yes', and when I'm not, I say 'No'.

WILFRED RHODES, explaining the secret of his excellent understanding over short singles with Jack Hobbs.

SAM Cook (during one of many running mix-ups): Call, Bomber!
'BOMBER' Wells (his Gloucestershire team-mate): 'Heads!

Let's cut out some of the quick singles.
OK, Ken, we'll cut out yours.

EXCHANGE between Ken Barrington and Fred Titmus towards end of a hot day in Australia.

WE'LL get 'em in singles.

GEORGE HIRST to Wilfred Rhodes (apocryphal), before last-wicket stand of 15 for England to beat Australia at The Oval, **1902**.

Go back, sergeant!

THE COMMAND was from Major Ridley; the sergeant, who was run out, was Sergeant Ayling; the order ensured that the Second Royal Surrey Militia were dismissed for nought by Shillinglea, Sussex, **1855**.

YOU'VE got more bloody edges than a broken pisspot.

FRED TRUEMAN to Northants batsman, **1956**.

YOU'RE not Ranji, so aim at mid-on's nut and you'll find the ball will go over the square-leg boundary.

SAMMY WOODS' advice to his Somerset colleagues, recorded in *Homes of Cricket*, George Plumptre, **1988**.

I never wanted to make a hundred. Who wants to make a hundred anyway? When I first went in, my immediate objective was to hit the ball to each of the four corners of the field. After that I tried not to be repetitive.

SIR LEARIE CONSTANTINE, speech to Royal Commonwealth Society, **1963**.

I watch that video sometimes and it still seems make-believe. When Dilley and I were in we laughed and joked, seeing who could play the most idiotic stroke.

IAN BOTHAM on famous victory against Australia in Headingley Test, **1981**, from *It Sort of Clicks*, Botham and Peter Roebuck, **1986**.

RUNS kept coming and I cast care aside and hit harder.

EDWIN ALLETSON's description of his 189 in 90 minutes for Notts at Hove in **1911**.

I didn't even know the record existed. I just kept going.

GRAEME HICK after scoring 405 not out for Worcestershire *v* Somerset, 19 short of A. C. MacLaren's record first-class score in England, **1988**.

No man on this earth could ever get 300 runs in a day if the opposition set out to contain him.

DON BRADMAN, discussing his achievement of that feat, BBC Radio, **1966**.

I'VE never seen any bugger get 300 in a day.

BRIAN CLOSE on Ken Rutherford's innings of 317 during the **1986** Scarborough Festival.

I hate defensive strokes – you only get three off them.

W. G. GRACE.

EVERY ball was labelled: either 1, 2, 3, 4, or 6. I leave out the 5. Too damn far to run.

CHARLIE MACARTNEY, from *Fingleton on Cricket*, **1972**.

ON the legside of the wicket lay safety; on the off the surgery windows. Small wonder, therefore, if a pronounced penchant for the 'pull' should have affected my batting throughout my days.

G. L. JESSOP on cricket at home in a small garden with attendant punishment for breaking his father's windows.

THE cover drive is the most beautiful stroke in batsmanship. Does that throw any light on why I am a self-admitted lover of all things British and traditional?

COLIN COWDREY in *MCC*, **1976**.

THE cut was never a business stroke.

WILFRED RHODES.

WHEN next I come to play against the Gentlemen of Lincolnshire I shall bring a broom-handle.

W. G. GRACE replying to a post-match toast at Grimsby. He had scored his regular hundred after apparently being out first ball.

FENDER . . . gave some amusement by hitting Armstrong back-handed on the off-side for a couple.

PELHAM WARNER reporting in *The Cricketer*, England *v* Australia, Old Trafford, **1921**. The first reverse sweep?

WHAT do I think of the reverse sweep? It's like Manchester United getting a penalty and Bryan Robson taking it with his head.

DAVID LLOYD, former England opening batsman.

IT's always a good idea to aim the first ball right here at the bowler's head. They don't like it. It rattles 'em.

CHARLIE MACARTNEY in *Fingleton on Cricket*, **1972**.

KILLICK was almost frightened to bowl. I don't think he minded his bowling being hit so much as he was worried Ted might hit one back at him.

JOHN GUNN on Edwin Alletson's 189 in 90 minutes for Notts at Hove, **1911**.

IT was a hard, slow, rather dispiriting road, and for a long time the swinging ball filled me with the fear of God.

COLIN COWDREY on his early days with Kent.

A yorker, sir? I don't know. I never had one.

w. g. grace when asked for advice on playing yorkers.

I thought if I didn't go in tonight I'd never get in at all against that bowling.

grace's explanation for not sending in a night-watchman in difficult conditions.

You never intimidate a good player.

greg chappell in *Howzat*, **1980**.

None of us likes it [fast bowling] but some of us don't let on.

maurice leyland, England and Yorkshire batsman.

The best technique in the world is no use if you're backing away to square leg.

geoffrey boycott, coaching England batsmen in **1989**, on attributes they would need for forthcoming West Indies tour.

Good Lord, he's knocked old George off his horse now.

geoff arnold, watching from England's dressing room as Dennis Lillee hit Keith Fletcher on touring cap, MCC in Australia, **1974/5**.

No good hitting me there mate, nothing to damage.

derek randall, responding to being 'skulled' by Dennis Lillee in Centenary Test, Melbourne, **1977**.

I'll have quite a rugged countenance by the time I'm finished.

mike brearley, England captain, hit on the nose by Ghavri, Indian bowler, MCC *v* India at Lord's, **1980**.

He looks like a cuddly little panda.

tony brown, England's tour manager, assessing the damage done to Mike Gatting's nose by the West Indian quicks, **1986**.

DEAR Mum, things are looking up. Today I got a half-volley in the nets.

> DAVID LLOYD, Lancashire batsman, in letter home during Australian tour, **1972/3**.

TRULY, I think I could get more runs if England had some faster bowlers.

> VIV RICHARDS, **1976**.

JOHNNIE, if you ever get hit again, make sure you drop inside the crease.

> BRIAN CLOSE, advice to John Hampshire after he was poleaxed by a bouncer from Charlie Griffiths which gave him headaches for life, **1963**.

IT should be a cause of real concern to administrators that the batsman himself has become as much a target as the wickets he defends.

> WISDEN editorial, **1985**.

Do you wish to prefer charges?

> POLICE SERGEANT to Sri Lanka's Sunil Wettimuny, when he arrived bruised in hospital during World Cup, saying that 'Jeff Thomson did it', **1975**.

Is this a time for heroics or should we go off?
I'd eff off if I were you!

> EXCHANGE between John Barclay and Jeff Thomson after Thomson had hit Barclay on the helmet with a bouncer, **1985**.

I don't know why they bother to put the stumps out. None of those buggers are trying to hit them.

> GRAEME FOWLER after an uncomfortable two hours v West Indies, Oval Test, **1985**.

I always maintain it is time enough to get runs when the bell is round your throat on a little blue or pink ribbon, which means you have become a rabbit as far as your bowling is concerned.

> SAMMY WOODS.

I used to get bored with batting. All I ever wanted to do was bowl. I had one shot – the slog – and if I hit it, the ball went a long way and the crowd and I were happy. If I missed it, well I was that much closer to bowling.

'BOMBER' WELLS, Gloucestershire and Nottinghamshire off-spinner, in *The Spinner's Turn*, **1982**.

> . . . at last
> the bowler flails once more.
> a final twitch for the dying day.

JOHN SNOW in *Moments and Thoughts*, **1973**.

BY and large cricket is governed by a self-perpetuating oligarchy of willow wielders! On almost every committee and at most conferences batters comfortably outnumber the game's honest toilers!

ROBIN MARLAR, **1959**.

THE last bowler to be knighted was Sir Francis Drake.

ARTHUR MAILEY.

THERE is hardly one first-class amateur bowler in England, and in my opinion, laziness is one of the main causes of this, and another is the employment of professionals at schools and universities. I have never heard an amateur say, 'I am going to have a bowl'; it is always a 'knock'.

F. R. SPOFFORTH, **1906**.

No bowler could call himself a bowler unless he could bowl for two hours at a stretch.

ALFRED SHAW.

IT was often soul destroying. On wet wickets or slow ones, I was expected to charge up and down and let it go when I knew I had no earthly chance of getting anything out of the wicket.

JOHN SNOW, on the joys of bowling for Sussex, *Cricket Rebel*, **1976**.

FOR myself I should like 100 balls in the over.

ALFRED MYNN, the Lion of Kent, on the proposal to increase the over from 4 balls to 6.

COUNTY bowlers are nothing if not philosophical. I'll be there in midsummer, running up to Sir Geoffrey, convincing myself he's going to pad up to a straight one.

BRIAN BRAIN (Worcestershire, Gloucestershire), **1980**.

BOWLING which does not get men out, like batting which brings no runs to the score, is an art abused.

A. E. KNIGHT, *The Complete Cricketer*, **1906**.

THERE'S more in bowling than just turning your arm over. There's such a thing as observation.

WILFRED RHODES.

YOU can't flight a ball, only an over.

WILFRED RHODES.

THEORETICALLY every ball is a potential wicket-taker, but I relate bowling an over to having six shells in a gun. I use each one to manipulate the enemy into some sort of position where he's not sure and I can exploit him. So I might look for the fourth ball of a particular over to be the one with which I hope to get the batsman out.

RICHARD HADLEE, **1988**.

THE wicket was helpful, but I had to bowl and plan.

NARENDRA HIRWANI, Indian leg-spinner, after taking a record Test debut sixteen for 136 in Madras.

I suppose if I was to think every ball, they'd never get a run.

WILLIAM LILLYWHITE.

As I'm walking back I think maybe I'll bowl a googly. Then, as I run in, no, I'll bowl a leg-spinner. Then, do you know, just as I prepare to bowl, I decide it'll be a googly after all. And then, as I let go of the ball, I say, sod it, I'll bowl a top-spinner.

CHANDRASEKHAR, Indian spinner, on bowling method, as reported by Peter Roebuck in *It Sort of Clicks*, **1986**.

BILL, get a notebook. Put down everything you learn about the batsmen, the way they play, their best shots, their weakest shots. For ten years you'll learn something new every day. After that you'll remember something you've forgotten.

EMMOTT ROBINSON to the young Bill Bowes.

I never bowled at the wickets: I bowled at the stroke. I intended the batsman to make a stroke, then I tried to beat it. I tried to make the batsman move. The time a batsman makes mistakes is when he has to move his feet.

SYDNEY BARNES, **1953**.

I am not unhappy to be hit for six sixes. I want batsmen to play shots. Only then can I get them out.

BISHEN BEDI.

THE first victim was hit on the thumb and was led out bleeding profusely, his colleague fainted and the next man in decided not to bat.

HISTORY OF RADLEY COLLEGE, on W. E. W. Collins' feat of getting three batsmen with one delivery in the **1860s**.

THE practice of fast bowling in our schools and colleges is sadly, almost cruelly, neglected.

LILLYWHITE's article entitled 'The Decline of Fast Bowling', **1882**.

To bowl fast is to revel in the glad animal action, to thrill in physical power and to enjoy a certain sneaking feeling of superiority over the mortals who play the game.

FRANK TYSON in *A Typhoon Called Tyson*.

THE thicker you are, the better your chances of becoming a good quick bowler.

STEWART STOREY, Surrey coach, in *From the Nursery End*, **1985**.

MATURITY brings cunning to the fast bowler and adds yet another facet to his nature, other modes of attack to his repertoire. Yet the coming of guile to quick bowling can be like the advance of creeping paralysis to the body.

FRANK TYSON.

OUTWARDLY, thought and cunning methods add to the armoury of the quick bowler and make him the complete, shrewd, mechanically perfect athlete. Inwardly, guile saps the psychological foundations of the edifice of fast bowling until it takes away the real desire and very reasons for wanting to bowl quick.

FRANK TYSON.

THERE'S no sitting duck like a scared duck.

RAY LINDWALL.

SPEAKING as a one-time fast bowler, who was also on the distinctly short side of length, it does not take one long to spot the player . . . who is always fearing the worst. A fast bowler, when he has gained this unsettling influence, can scarcely be blamed if he plays up to it.

G. L. JESSOP.

WHEN [William] Barnes came in to bat, W.G., who wasn't captain . . . said to me 'keep 'em short'. I did and hit Barnes over the heart first ball. I think he got a two and then out. In the second innings I again kept them short and again hit him in the ribs. I apologised.

S. M. J. WOODS.

SORRY DOC, she slipped.

ERNEST JONES, Australian fast bowler, firing delivery through W. G. Grace's beard during rout of England, **1896**.

I used to give every new batsman four balls. One was a bouncer to check his courage, the second a fizzer to check his eyesight, the third was a slow 'un to try out his reflexes and the fourth a bender to see if he was a good cricketer. And if he took a single off each of the four balls, I knew I was in trouble.

HAROLD LARWOOD, **1972**.

REMEMBER, lad, one day we'll have a fast bowler – and I hope that day isn't far off.

LEN HUTTON to Ray Lindwall after some torrid overs, **1950/51**.

I shouldn't have done that.

RAY LINDWALL upon hitting Tyson with a bouncer during the Australia *v* England series, **1954/5**.

WHEN I was captain I always told my bowlers that if they bowled bumpers they'd have to expect a few in return. You can't expect that if you're scaring people half to death you're not going to get one or two bouncers around your ears, too.

CLIVE LLOYD, West Indies manager, as Australian Geoff Lawson had his jaw broken by Curtly Ambrose, Second Test, Perth, **1988**.

WE bowl short at them, they bowl short at us – it's as simple as that.

GEOFF LAWSON, after Ambrose's bouncer broke his jaw, **1988**.

AT 1.22 p.m. Lindwall bowled the first bumper. Immediately a clatter of typewriters broke out from the Press tent.

JACK FINGLETON, *The Ashes Crown the Year*, on first bouncer bowled on Australians' tour of England in **1953**.

I want to hit you Bailey – I want to hit you over the heart.

SOUTH AFRICAN pace bowler Peter Heine to Trevor Bailey.

WHEN tha's laikin' wi Fred, tha's not laikin' wi a soft ball, tha' knows.

FRED TRUEMAN in *Fast Fury*, **1961**.

I try to hit a batsman in the rib cage when I bowl a purposeful bouncer, and I want it to hurt so much that the batsman doesn't want to face me any more.

DENNIS LILLEE, *Back to the Mark*, **1974**.

I enjoy hitting a batsman more than getting him out. I like to see blood on the pitch. And I've been training on whisky.

JEFF THOMSON, **1974**.

I know I'm a ruthless bastard and I'll always have a go. But I wouldn't deliberately put a ball like that on anybody. It slipped. It honestly slipped.

DENNIS LILLEE, after a beamer to Bob Willis in Sydney, Australia *v* MCC, **1974/5** tour.

WHEN I hear Colin bowl de bounces, I get vex. Two bounces an over okay, but when he bowl five I get vex bad. I tell him, what happen if he hit batsman and he fall dead on de spot?

COLIN CROFT'S MOTHER, during England's tour of West Indies, **1981** (from *Cricket Wallah*, Scyld Berry, **1982**).

I don't want any bloody sympathy, do you understand that? It has happened. People who say 'I know how you feel' are just talking bullshit. They don't know, not at all. What I can't forget is that the ball was a deliberate short one. Not deliberately at his head, but still deliberate.

PETER LEVER, after felling Ewen Chatfield, New Zealand's No. 11, with a short delivery, Auckland Test **1975**. Chatfield was hit on the temple and his heart stopped for several seconds.

You look a sight worse than I do.

EWEN CHATFIELD, when Peter Lever visited him in Auckland Hospital, **1975**.

REMEMBER, with these speedsters bowling at 95 miles per hour, cricket can kill.

AUSTRALIAN TV ADVERT for Packer Circus, **1977**.

SIR – 'Cricket' used to be a synonym for honourable conduct. It is now becoming a synonym for brute force. Is it not time that respected leaders in all countries spoke out?

LORD BROCKWAY, letter to the *Guardian* on short-pitched fast bowling, **1975**.

ENGLAND'S pace bowlers are making the helmet go out of fashion.

SCYLD BERRY, the *Observer*, **1981**.

THIS is our weapon now, so we have got to use it.

VIV RICHARDS on West Indies' possession of a powerful speed attack.

I have never felt it more likely that we should see someone killed.

JOHN WOODCOCK, in *The Times*, following England's mauling by West Indies pace bowlers, Kingston Test, **1986**.

WITHIN a decade every top team will field four fast bowlers pitching short with no-one in front of the bat. Adventurous batting will be reserved for one day games. Ruthlessness and violence will be indistinguishable.

PETER ROEBUCK, *Sydney Morning Herald,* **1989**.

THE retaliation is simple and straightforward. Having successfully (?) evaded the high-head bouncer the batsman should feel entitled to straighten up, go into a hammer-thrower's crouch and hurl his bat at the bowler just completing his follow-through. This to me sounds fair game.

PETER WALKER'S suggestion for countering the proliferation of bouncers, **1962**.

THE applause from the slips that greets anything banged in half-way has retarded the progress of at least two promising seamers.

MIKE SELVEY, former Middlesex medium-fast bowler, on the county's approach under Mike Gatting's captaincy, **1988**.

THERE is a feeling among some batsmen that bowlers should ping it in.

JON AGNEW on his failure to regain an England place after cutting down his pace and taking 100 wickets in **1988**.

IN 1980 I had a lot of injury problems – ankles, hamstrings. I couldn't handle running in from 25 yards five or six days a week. So I made a dramatic change in my technique and scaled my run-up down by half. It meant I had to go back to fundamentals and start again with my timing and rhythm. Since then my strike rates have been twice as effective and consistent, I can bowl longer spells, and movement of the ball is greater than it's ever been in the past.

RICHARD HADLEE, **1988**.

Do you want three slips and a gully, or four slips?
Who do you think I am, Malcolm Marshall?

EXCHANGE between Mark Nicholas and his opening bowler Arnie Sidebottom, MCC v Australia **1985**.

As I grew older, the elastic snapped. I lost the pace, the zip and the sting had gone. I remember taking two catches off my own bowling against Glamorgan and being complimented on my cleverly disguised slower ball.

TED DEXTER, *Wisden Cricket Monthly*, **1980**.

THAT season [1897] was the first in which the idea that the ball could be made to swing in the air appeared to us as a workable proposition.

G. L. JESSOP.

I shall bowl the first ball but I don't know about a full over. I can't really spin 'em now. I can cut 'em, of course, but any fool can do that.

SYDNEY BARNES, bowling first over of match to mark his 80th birthday, Barnes's XI v England XI, **1953**.

IF I came into the game now, I'd probably end up as a medium-pace dobber.

FRED TITMUS, former England off-spinner, **1982**.

THE mentality of the medium-pace bowler as a general rule does not rate up to that of the more subtle type of bowler.

ARTHUR MAILEY.

WITH very few exceptions the great spin bowlers of cricket were personalities and men of character – not always pleasant but invariably interesting. They may have lacked the charm and friendliness of their faster confederates; they may have been more temperamental and less self-disciplined; but there seemed to be an absence of orthodoxy about them and they were able to meander through life as individuals not as civil servants.

ARTHUR MAILEY.

SLOW bowling is an art, Mr Kelly, and art is international.

ARTHUR MAILEY replying to a reprimand from the Australian manager for giving advice to England leg-break bowler Ian Peebles on the **1930** tour, Manchester Test.

BEST ball on a sticky pitch is a spinnin' half-volley.

WILFRED RHODES.

WHEN a spinner comes on, your eyes go round like dollar signs on a fruit machine. Everyone wants to hit him because they can't smash the fast bowler.

ALLAN LAMB, England batsman, **1982**.

BATSMEN'S technique against spin has improved out of all proportion. Trevor Bailey writes about the immaculate control of Bill O'Reilly and Clarrie Grimmett. How would they fare after being smeared over extra from leg stump or shovelled over square leg from outside off?

SIMON HUGHES, Middlesex fast bowler, **1988**.

'ARE there any spinners playing?' asked one Leicester spectator. 'Don't mock the afflicted,' said his mate. Afflicted they certainly are. Balls keep their shine longer (with or without the application of lip gloss) so are harder to grip, and rippling muscles and chunky bats mean slow bowlers get hit much further.

SIMON HUGHES, Middlesex fast bowler, **1988**.

ONE general and melancholy fact may indeed be noticed here. No less than five of the six leading counties have found it necessary to begin their attack with slow bowlers. . . . The causes of this dreary and monotonous prevalence of slow bowling are many and amongst the most noteworthy may be cited the extraordinary and exaggerated excellence of grounds, the immense number of first-class matches which the increased facilities of locomotion have brought into existence and, lastly, the absolute mastery which, for five or six years, Mr W. G. Grace acquired over fast bowling.

LILLYWHITE'S CRICKETERS' COMPANION, about **1880** season.

IT's all a matter of inches – those between your ears.

ARTHUR MILTON on spin bowling, **1982**.

THE great thing about spin bowling is that it is an art which can be learnt. In that sense it is different from fast bowling. A fast bowler either has the natural ability to hurl the ball down quickly or he hasn't. And if he can't do it, there is no way you can coach it into him. The reverse is true of spin bowling. I believe you can learn it from scratch.

RAY ILLINGWORTH in *Spin Bowling*, **1980**.

IF a batsman thinks it's spinning, then it's spinning.

WILFRED RHODES in Neville Cardus, *Autobiography*, **1947**.

IT's all tommy-rot this talk about dropping a ball on a sixpence. Let 'em try and hit a kitchen hearth-rug.

TED PEATE, Yorkshire slow left-armer, **1880s**, whose accuracy was legendary.

TRY the morning paper.

WILFRED RHODES' gloss on Peate's statement.

IT must be very humiliating for any skipper to see balls bouncing twice, with full pitches and long hops thrown in as a matter of course.

A. C. MACLAREN on googly bowling.

POOR old googly! It has been subjected to ridicule, abuse, contempt, incredulity, and survived them all.

B. J. T. BOSANQUET, inventor of the googly, *Wisden*, **1924**.

IT was rather a pity Ellis got run out at 1107, because I was just striking a length.

ARTHUR MAILEY after taking four for 362 while Victoria scored 1107 *v* New South Wales, **1926**.

I remember playing in dozens of matches with Douglas Wright when he should never have been in the side. Not only did we find ourselves playing with ten men, but with every over of honest toil he was driving another nail into our own coffin.

COLIN COWDREY.

IT's always a blow when anyone who propels a ball at less than 50 m.p.h. calls it a day.

JON AGNEW regretting the retirement of Vic Marks and Jack Simmons in **1989**.

GENTLEMEN, I think you might put me in on Monday morning and get me out by about Saturday night.

FULLER PILCH, asked his opinion of underhand bowling, **1820s**.

WHEN I've bowled the ball, I've done with her and leaves her to my field.

WILLIAM LILLYWHITE.

IT can therefore be laid down as an absolute principle in team selection that the best wicket-keeper, irrespective of all other considerations, should always be chosen.

MCC COACHING MANUAL.

I should like this man to be of a grave demeanour and humble mind.

MOHUMMUD ABDULLAH KHAN on wicket-keepers, *Introduction to Cricket Guide*, **1891**.

YOU must rinse your hands in the chamberpot every day. The urine hardens them wonderfully.

HERBERT STRUDWICK, the former England wicket-keeper, offering advice to A. G. Pawson of Oxford University.

I shall have to catch a later train tonight – that one knocked off the 7.30.

FRED STEDMAN, predecessor of Strudwick as Surrey wicket-keeper, who used a copy of the South Western Railway timetable as protection after he was hit in the chest.

THERE are three reasons I can be wicket-keeping badly . . . lack of concentration, standing up too soon, or snatching at the ball. The longer you stay crouching, even for a thousandth of a second, may mean the difference between the ball glancing off your finger or sticking in the middle of your glove.

BOB TAYLOR, **1985**.

He did not wait for the ball off the wicket from which to perform his leg-glide stunt, but persisted in persuading the straight ball to take the outside course.' G. L. Jessop on Ranji (*above left*)

'One of the dirtiest necks I have ever kept wicket behind.' Lord Cobham on W. G. Grace (*above right*)

There's no ruddy best ball to bowl at the Don.' Bill Voce on Bradman. *Below*, Bradman demonstrates the point

'The drums, I miss the drums' said Viv Richards. A West Indies band takes the field during a bomb scare in the days before steel bands were banned

'He (Merv Hughes) will probably be brought to England either as a fast bowler, a mascot or as a folk hero. He shouldn't take wickets or score runs. But then he shouldn't have done so in Perth or Adelaide either. He is a bloke, if not a cricketer, to be reckoned with.' Peter Roebuck, 1989. *Below*, Merv Hughes bowling to Jack Russell during the 1st Test at Headingley in 1989

'He looks like a cuddly little Panda.' Tony Brown, England tour manager, assessing the effects of Gatting's meeting with Michael Holding, West Indies *v* England, 1986 (*above left*)

'Ian gave 120 per cent on the field, but he only ever had 50–80 per cent of his ability to give because he was never fit. He turned up for training only a couple of times, and the coach, Ray Reynolds, said it was better he didn't come because he was a disruptive influence when he was there.' Greg Chappell. *Above right*, Botham gives his all in training with Worcestershire

'The wicket was river-bed silt – low and slow.' Graeme Fowler on the Gauhati wicket (*below right*)

'I think Gatting's dispute with Shakoor Rana did a major disservice to English cricket. Is it worthwhile going on unless we restore values for the benefit of the next generation.' Ossie Wheatley, chairman TCCB committee, explaining his veto on Gatting's captaincy. *Above left*, the incident that started it all

'There was a social prejudice against the scorer who was a descendant of the baggage man.' Vic Isaacs, Hampshire scorer. *Above right*, Isaacs scoring (*right*) for Derby *v* Hants at Heanor, 1987

'I think it's only fair that the world should know that Ted and Micky wanted Gatting. They have taken a lot of stick and it's right that the record should be put straight.' Ossie Wheatley, chairman TCCB committee, confirming that Gower had been the second choice as captain *v* Australia, 1989. *Below*, the captain and his reluctant advisers

A wicket-keeper who is on his toes is likely to overbalance.

C. B. PONSONBY (Worcestershire, **1920s**).

A slack, careless fielder needs the stick: he cannot possibly have a right and proper spirit.

RANJITSINHJI, *The Jubilee Book of Cricket*, **1897**.

I just put my hand down as a pretence, which pleases the crowd, taking good care never to touch the ball, which pleases me, and so everybody is satisfied.

GEORGE GIFFEN (South Australia) giving advice to Charles McLeod (Victoria) after the latter had injured himself stopping Giffen's fierce straight drive.

THE ball fizzed through the fielders as if they had been ghosts. I have never seen another innings like it. One of those drives would have smashed a man's hand if he had tried to stop it.

GEORGE GUNN, Notts batsman, on Alletson's innings, 189 in 90 minutes for Notts against Sussex in **1911**.

THE fielders must take especial care not to exchange jokes with one another, or try funny tricks, that do secretly divide their attention and produce a horrible defect in their fielding.

MOHUMMUD ABDULLAH KHAN, *Introduction to Cricket Guide*, **1891**.

I only just have to perch myself at short leg and just stare at some of 'em to get 'em out. They fiddle about and look away and then they look back to see if I'm staring at 'em. I am. They don't stay long.

BRIAN CLOSE.

THEE get on with thi laikin', and I'll get on wi' mine.

EMMOTT ROBINSON, of Yorkshire, warned he was in danger fielding close to bat.

BE ready for rebounds!

BRIAN CLOSE (short square) to Ray East (forward short leg).

THE only thing which I'm very keen to do before I leave Somerset is to throw myself at the ball, and to dive, as I see the other team-mates in the Somerset team do. And I'm sure when I do, when I really do dive, I'm going to get a big applause.

SUNIL GAVASKAR, BBC Eastern Service, **1980**.

THERE'S an epidemic around here, but it isn't catching.

TOM EMMETT, suffering a spate of dropped catches.

IT wasn't the light that bothered me so much as the pounding of my heart as the ball came down.

GRAEME FOWLER, Lancashire, on the catch in the gloom that ended Trevor Jesty's innings for Hampshire and took Lancashire into the **1986** NatWest final.

AFTER working all day I just go down to the river and catch the swallows as they flit by.

G. J. BONNOR (Australia) explaining his ability as a slip. Sammy Woods said he didn't believe the yarn, but he added that Bonnor, who was 6'5", 'had very long arms'.

WHEN I was quite young I made a boy, when out for a walk, throw stones into a hedge, and as the sparrows flew out, I caught 'em.

F. R. SPOFFORTH, Australian fast bowler, explaining his skill at slip. (Related by 'Buns' Thornton, *Wisden*, **1927**.)

5

The Beautiful Game

Styles, Standards and Lifestyles

THE whole edifice of the Christian virtues could be raised on a basis of good cricket.

EDWARD CRACOFT LACEY, **1800s**.

A chance to play the man and act the gentleman.

SIR FREDERICK TOONE on cricket, *Wisden*, **1930**.

CRICKET is not only a game but a school of the greatest social importance.

LORD HARRIS.

THERE is one sentiment which sways every true player and every good man, and it is this – that in all the religious, political and secular affairs of life, as well as in every match, may the best side win.

AN OLD CAMBRIDGE CAPTAIN, *Wisden*, **1895**.

YE gods, is the game to be ruled by young men, some of whom are prepared to take the unwritten law into their own hands?

LORD HAWKE, following first artificial declaration in first-class cricket, Gloucestershire *v* Yorkshire, **1931**.

THE counties will soon be captained by computers.

JOHN WOODCOCK, *The Times*, aghast at the growing number of negotiated declarations in county cricket, **1986**.

You do well to love it, for it is more free from anything sordid, anything dishonourable than any game in the world. To play it keenly, honourably, generously, self-sacrificingly is a moral lesson in itself, and the class-room is full of God's air and sunshine. Foster it, my brothers, so that it may attract all who can find the time to play it; protect it from anything that would sully it, so that it may grow in favour with all men.

LORD HARRIS's speech to half-holiday cricketers, quoted in letter to *The Times* on his 80th birthday, **1931**.

WHAT can you have better than a nice green field, with the wickets set up, and to go out and do the best for your side?

GEORGE HIRST in his retirement speech at Scarborough, **1921**.

In Affectionate Remembrance
of
ENGLISH CRICKET
which died at the Oval
on
29th August, 1882.

Deeply lamented by a large circle of
Sorrowing Friends and Acquaintances
R.I.P.
N.B. – The body will be cremated, and the
Ashes taken to Australia.

SPORTING TIMES obituary which began the story of 'The Ashes'.

IN affectionate remembrance of English Cricket which died at Lord's on September 2, 1980, aged one hundred. The body will be re-cremated and sent to the home of bureaucracy, officialdom, and the tactics of defensive unadventurous cricket.

LETTER in *Wisden Cricket Monthly*.

TOUCH the Ashes and hidden spears will come out of the walls.

COLONEL JOHN STEPHENSON, MCC Secretary, on suggestion that Lord's security was vulnerable, **1988**.

To some people cricket is a circus show upon which they may or may not find it worthwhile to spend sixpence; to others it is a pleasant means of livelihood; to others a physical fine art full of plot, interest and enlivened by difficulties; to others in some sort it is a cult and a philosophy.

C. B. FRY, Foreword to D. L. A. Jephson's *A Few Overs*, 1913.

CRICKET is indescribable. How do you describe an orgasm?

GREG MATTHEWS (Australia).

IF you have a right ambition, you will desire to excel all boys at cricket as well as in learning.

LORD CHESTERFIELD in a letter to his son, then at Eton, 1740s.

PERSONALLY, I have always looked upon cricket as organised loafing.

WILLIAM TEMPLE, later Archbishop of Canterbury and then headmaster of Repton School, 1925.

CRICKET is the only game that you can actually put on weight when playing.

TOMMY DOCHERTY, former football manager, on Piccadilly Radio, 1990.

THE very word 'cricket' has become a synonym for all that is true and honest. To say 'that is not cricket' implies something under-hand, something not in keeping with the best ideals.

SIR PELHAM WARNER.

I'M convinced that what the public want are heroic performances and chivalrous conduct. And like most of them, I don't believe winning is everything.

TED DEXTER on his appointment as Chairman of the England committee, 1989.

CRICKET and citizenship are synonymous.

KEITH ANDREW, head of NCA coaching and former England wicket-keeper, 1986.

To play cricket is synonymous with running straight.

EARL OF DERBY at Lancashire's Championship Dinner, **1926**.

IN a desperate state of the game, every manoeuvre must be tried.

JOHN NYREN.

ANY device or excuse is legitimate that may delay the game and the strikers thus become cold and inactive.

JOHN NYREN advocating gamesmanship to disturb strikers' concentration.

ONE could not be too particular when playing twenty-two.

TOM LOCKYER, All England XI wicket-keeper, replying to criticism for tricking an opponent into leaving his ground.

USE every weapon within the rules, and stretch the rules to breaking point, I say.

FRED TRUEMAN, **1961**.

WE are perfectly entitled to prepare a surface which suits us and makes it more difficult for them. When England go to the West Indies next winter we have to take the type of pitches they give us – and you can be quite sure they will not be turners.

GEOFFREY BOYCOTT, **1981**.

FIXING pitches to suit the best bowlers of the home side seems to be the trend these days. I don't mind, but I hope nobody knocks us in future when we prepare wickets for our guys.

VIV RICHARDS after West Indies were greeted with a slow turner at Old Trafford in **1988**. They won anyway.

THE English have the irritating habit of appealing in chorus at every possible opportunity, presumably with the motive of discommoding the batsman. The sooner this undesirable habit is corrected the better.

ADELAIDE ADVERTISER, on Shrewsbury's England team in Australia, **1884**.

THE team was also urged to improve its appealing, an area in which the Australians are undoubtedly superior. When appealing, the Australians make a statement; we ask a question.

VIC MARKS, Somerset and England all-rounder, describing team meeting during tour of Australia, **1982/3**.

BEHAVE like 'gentlemen' after the game is over, avoid clapping and laughing in faces of the persons you have defeated.

MOHUMMUD ABDULLAH KHAN, *Introduction to Cricket Guide*, **1891**.

JUST remember one thing son, you've already been killed once on a cricket field.

IAN BOTHAM'S warning to Ewen Chatfield after the New Zealand seamer had run out Derek Randall while Randall was backing up, Christchurch Test, **1977/8** tour.

WHEN Randall was run out backing up I thought that if it had been my school the bowler would have been beaten for it by the housemaster – and quite right too.

PHIL EDMONDS on New Zealand *v* England, **1977/8**.

YOU know a few Afrikaans swear words. Have a go at him.

IAN BOTHAM to Allan Lamb during Wessels' 162, Australia *v* England, Brisbane, **1982/3**.

I don't think we have met – my name's Cowdrey.

COLIN COWDREY, pressed into service on England's **1974** tour of Australia, introducing himself at the crease to the tearaway pace bowler, Jeff Thomson.

WHICHEVER side it may be – and I fancy Eton were the principal offenders – the growing tendency towards ebullitions of affectionate exuberance in the field must be severely checked. They are not pretty at Wembley, but at Lord's quite intolerable.

'GHMC' on Eton *v* Harrow, *The Cricketer*, **1955**.

IF you all hate Harrow, clap your hands!

ETON BOYS at Lord's, **1986**.

WE report misdemeanours and nothing happens. Players always seem able to find a way round regulations today if they want to.

DAVID ARCHER, West Indian umpire, **1988**.

EYES to the front, shut up, or you will be next.

IAN BOTHAM to a passenger protesting at his assault on another passenger, Adrian Winter, who had objected to Botham's language on an internal Australian flight, **1988**. Botham was fined £320.

HE just happened to be on the wrong plane at the wrong time.

BOTHAM on Winter.

TEST Stars in Sex Orgy.

THE *SUN* front page headline on 8 June which broke the story leading to the sacking of Mike Gatting after the First Test *v* West Indies, **1988**.

THE selectors emphasised that they did not believe the allegations [of sexual frolics] in the newspapers and accepted Gatting's account of what happened. The selectors were concerned, however, that Gatting behaved irresponsibly during a Test match by inviting female company to his room for a drink in the late evening.

SELECTORS' statement upon removing Gatting from the England captaincy.

IF they deny the allegations we will accept their word as well. We do not regard this as a whitewash.

MICKY STEWART, England team manager, announcing that four other players would be interviewed at Lord's about the Nottingham hotel frolics. All denied involvement.

THE selectors asked for an explanation, which I gave. They tell me they believe my version of the events, even issuing a statement saying so – and then sack me. I couldn't believe it.

MIKE GATTING on the barmaid affair which cost him the captaincy in **1988**.

IF chairman of selectors Peter May *et al.* are genuinely concerned about Gatting's bringing the game into disrepute, then surely the image flashed across the world of an England captain poking a Pakistani umpire in the chest would have been a far better reason to sack him. But oh no! For that disgraceful tour the TCCB not only failed to axe the captain, they even voted the lads an extra £1000 bonus into the bargain. On the basis of that sort of lunacy, the average cricketer might even be forgiven for expecting a couple of hundred quid for bonking the odd barmaid.

FRANCES EDMONDS on Gatting's dismissal, *Mail on Sunday,* **1988**.

THERE will be an extremely strict code. Rule number one: that they are extremely good-looking ladies.

TED DEXTER's philosophy on a Test cricketer's social behaviour, expressed shortly before becoming chairman of the England committee, **1989**.

IF a young bachelor player spends some time with a smart lady, returns to the hotel in good time and then ends up in the tabloid press, I'm likely to commiserate, and even congratulate. But good clean fun and late-night revelry are two different things. Nothing that is illegal, immoral or offensive can be condoned.

DEXTER's more considered view on the same, **1989**.

INNOVATIONS invariably are suspect, and in no quarter more so than the cricket world.

G. L. JESSOP.

THESE bowlers might run people out, or stump them out, or catch them out, but they can't bowl to bowl anyone out; that bowling isn't mediogrity [sic]!

WILLIAM LILLYWHITE on the bowlers of **1840s/50s**.

IN those days bowlers bowled a length for batsmen to make strokes, and such rubbish as leg theories on perfect wickets was not indulged in then.

A. C. MACLAREN on Tom Richardson's unchanged 3¼-hour spell of six for 76 in 42.3 overs as Australia scored 125–7 *v* England at Old Trafford, **1896**.

OVER after over was bowled outside the off-stump in the hope that the batsman would make a mistake. Some did; others, profiting by experience, refused to be led into temptation, and consequently some very boresome periods eventuated.

G. L. JESSOP on the same period.

THEY now look for clowns, not cricketers.

SYDNEY BARNES on northern leagues' increasing stress on 'showman' professionals, **1929**.

THIS will be the pinnacle of my career. It has always been my ambition to play in the Central Lancashire League.

RAVI RATNAYEKE, Sri Lankan Test player, on joining Todmorden, **1988**.

YOU don't know anything about it; it's a different game today.

YORKSHIRE PLAYER to retired seam bowler Tony Nicholson, **1981**.

WHEN the old hands complain that the batsmen of their day would have murdered Ramadhin and put Laker on the defensive they have right on their side. Their only mistake was to believe that that style of play can be invoked at will. It was more than a method, it was a philosophy of life.

C. L. R. JAMES, *Beyond a Boundary*, **1963**.

THE gap in application between the earlier greats and their lesser contemporaries was far, far greater than the one between today's Test and county cricketers. It is not that modern top-line cricketers are inferior to their predecessors, it is that the post-war average county cricketer has raised his game.

PETER WALKER, *The Cricketer*, **1963**.

FOR thorough enjoyment, Test matches were too deadly serious. One always had the feeling of sitting on a barrel of gunpowder in contiguity to a lighted match and at the mercy of an untoward puff of wind.

G. L. JESSOP.

MOST people looking at the game from the outside cannot hope to appreciate the strain involved. Each Test match is a week full of pressure. I notice it more when new players join the England side. Take Les Taylor – he is a very experienced cricketer, yet the transition to Test level took him by surprise. He felt a difference in the atmosphere and tension, and like all newcomers found himself drained of energy more quickly than usual.

DAVID GOWER, **1985**.

IN the Tests I sometimes break out into a sweat just putting on me boots. You'd be really surprised at how many players are nervous out there.

MIKE HENDRICK.

I don't actually enjoy Test cricket that much.

CHRIS TAVARÉ after making 35 runs in 5½ hours at Madras, England tour of India, **1981/ 2**.

THE image of the West Indian game is different now. The fellows are more professional and there is so much cricket being played that the joy has been taken out of the game. Twenty years ago we were the frivolous calypso cricketers. Now the players just tend to go out and do a job.

JACKIE HENDRIKS, West Indies manager and former wicket-keeper, **1988**.

A day will come when an England captain will appear in the dock at the Old Bailey, charged with doing less than his best.

COLIN COWDREY on the pressures of the modern game in the aftermath of the Gatting affair, **1988**.

Too much cricket will kill cricketers before they are ready to be killed.

MIKE GATTING, **1987**.

IT puts a lot of pressure on the chaps to train 365 days a year to play just one Test match.

RANJAN MADUGALLE, Sri Lanka captain, on his side's problems, **1988**.

I think I could write a sort of Egon Ronay guide to casualty departments – a kind of Good Hospital Guide.

GRAHAME CLINTON, Surrey opener, injured on grounds in 15 of the 17 first-class counties, **1986**. (From *Wisden Cricket Monthly*.)

THE fact that cricket has to be left off during the winter months may be the reason for the fatality which seems to attend professional cricketers: they seldom live long.

JAMES CANTLIE, *Physical Efficiency*, **1906**.

A Test match contest is no kid-glove affair, and as a bat is a weapon of defence as well as attack, a first-class batsman, especially on modern-day wickets, should be able to deal safely with fast bowling, no matter of how short a length.

G. L. JESSOP, *The Cricketer*, **1921**.

THIS is a Test match. It's not Old Reptonians versus Lymeswold, one off the mark and jolly good show.

DAVID GOWER, England's captain, refusing to condemn Malcolm Marshall's use of bouncers during Fifth Test *v* West Indies, **1984**.

BEFORE they went in C. T. Studd was walking round the pavilion with a blanket over him; A. G. Steel's teeth were all in a chatter; and Billy Barnes's teeth would have been had he not left them at home.

TED PEATE on the scene in England's dressing room during the fourth innings of the Test, **1882**. Asked to score 85, England lost by 2 runs!

I couldn't trust Mr Studd.

TED PEATE. Yorkshire professional and No. 11, last out, having a slog, in the same match. Studd was, to some, one of the best amateur batsmen of the time.

THERE are 250 players in county cricket. All are on first name terms, all know the other 249's strengths and faults in the techniques of the game, and play on these failings, thus resulting in lower totals more slowly accumulated.

PETER WALKER (Glamorgan, England), **1961**.

THERE is an enormous amount of mediocrity in English cricket. A lot of very average players are making their living out of the game when really they shouldn't be in it.

RICHARD HADLEE in *At the Double*, **1985**.

COUNTY cricketers are a cautious lot. Though they've scored runs throughout their careers they do not trust their luck. They construct a technique in which imagination plays no part. Everything is tight, everything is predictable.

PETER ROEBUCK in *It Sort of Clicks*, Roebuck and Ian Botham, **1986**.

I sense a lower level of satisfaction than I would want among many English players at Test and county level. Players settle for just enough to get another contract.

BOBBY SIMPSON, **1989**.

CRICKET is a job, and they have played so long that they are basically fairly bored by it all. Most of them go through the seasons complaining it's too hot, or too cold, or too wet, or that the wicket is too slow, or too fast, and never in their favour, and so on and so forth. Anything new is deeply disliked – one-day cricket, for example, or team stretching exercises before the match, or overseas cricketers. Coloured overseas cricketers are particularly disliked since the 'old pros' are usually slightly racist.

IMRAN KHAN, *All Round View*, **1988**, on county cricket's 'old pros'.

THEY tended to enjoy horse racing, and the suspension of play due to rain. Without any doubt the best hours of the day for them were spent in the pub after the day's play. During home matches they could only spend a couple of hours in the pub, but on away matches, the entire evening might be spent there – after the customary 'clocking-in' phone call to the wife.

IMRAN KHAN, *All Round View*.

All cricketers have large egos. That is why there are so many below-average players still in the game. Each player secretly believes that he is a better cricketer than perhaps his results show.

PETER WALKER.

THE pest of the cricket field is the man who bores you about his average – his wickets – his catches; and looks blue even at the success of his own party. If unsuccessful in batting or fielding, he 'shuts up' – 'the wretch concentrated all in self'.

REV. JAMES PYCROFT, *The Cricket Field*, **1851**.

PLAYERS cannot be as selfish as they used to. Before, people used to play in order to be satisfied with their own performance. These days, you pick a team of workers and you would beat the teams of the past that had five stars who did it all.

JACK BOND, Lancashire team manager, **1985**.

ENGLAND won't improve in world terms until the younger players rediscover some professional pride.

BOB TAYLOR in *Standing Up, Standing Back*, **1985**.

THE modern cricketer is not an ogre, nor is he deliberately obstructive. Although in most cases it would be unfair to dismiss him as a spoiled brat, he is too often lazy, ill-disciplined and reluctant to put in the effort and dedication commensurate with the wages he is earning. He has a very low boredom threshold with a constant need to be told what to do with his time.

BOB WILLIS in *Lasting the Pace*, **1985**.

I saw them all around me on the county circuit – guys who are just playing for next year's contract. The batsmen do just enough to creep to 1000 runs in the season. The bowlers will sneak to the fifty-wicket mark. Then they feel safe. But it's not enough. With more concentration, more effort, and above all more pride in their performance, these same players could get 1200 runs or sixty wickets and maybe give their side a chance to win something instead of just marking time.

RICHARD HADLEE, **1988**.

YOUNG players used to come up the hard way, bowling to senior pros in the nets and cleaning their boots. Now everything is laid on for them, including sponsored cars. It's all too easy. Standards are nowhere near as high as when I first came to England.

RICHARD HADLEE on his retirement from county cricket in **1987**.

I am not necessarily forecasting success for England. There is no reason why, in a country where it is often impossible to have building work done or a motor car serviced properly, its sporting tradesmen should perform any better.

GRAEME WRIGHT, *Wisden* editor, previewing the **1989** season.

IN the ten years I was at Notts, only a couple of young players ever approached me for advice. I find that amazing, and it's an insight into the modern attitude. Maybe some guy has learned a bit from watching me, but as far as talking to me about technique and attitude, forget it. Nobody ever wanted to know.

RICHARD HADLEE, **1988**.

A coach who suppresses natural instincts may find that he has lifted a poor player to a mediocre one but has reduced a potential genius to the rank and file.

SIR DON BRADMAN, **1967**.

IF style counts for anything (and who really would attempt to deny it?), it simply must be insisted upon; in which case, in nine instances out of ten – bang goes individualism.

MAJOR G. A. FAULKNER, South African player and cricket coach. *The Cricketer*, **1925**.

I find it mystifying that England produces any cricketers at all.

COLIN MCCOOL on English coaching.

I was never coached; I was never told how to hold a bat.

SIR DON BRADMAN.

IN 20 years' cricket I only received half an hour of one-to-one tuition. That is ridiculous.

MICKY STEWART, England team manager, before **1989** Ashes humiliation.

I'VE lost more good players through interfering parents than for any other reason.

COLIN PAGE, Kent coach, in *From the Nursery End*, **1985**.

THE nets will be up, but don't expect our fellows to use them too much. They will be afraid of being jeered at by the men in the tramcars.

W. FINDLAY, Surrey secretary, **1915**. (Source: *Wisden*, **1917**.)

I feel petrified in nets. It makes me feel like one of those ducks at the fairground.

IAN BOTHAM, nationwide speaking tour, **1989**.

WE try to maintain the intensity of practice. You still rely on the willingness of the individual.

BOBBY SIMPSON, **1989.**

MEN are too often picked for a Test match on the strength of a hundred on a 'doped' pitch.

PATSY HENDREN, Middlesex and England batsman, *Wisden*, **1938**.

IN 1949, the decree went out that county groundsmen should strive to prepare more sporting wickets, in the belief that the *shirt-front* type of wicket was responsible for much of the dull cricket of the day. Little did people realise that this decision was to be the death-knell of the wrist-spinner, who must always be more expensive than the good finger spinner.

COLIN COWDREY, *The Cricketer*, **1963**.

ALREADY the press are lamenting on the paucity of new faces among the bowling fraternity. Any wonder – what youngster in his right mind gladly looks forward to a life of little glamour, few rewards and days of being just 'cannon-fodder' for opposing batsmen?

PETER WALKER on the **1958/62** experiment with covered wickets.

WHAT the legislators failed to take into account was that the average county player just has not the ability to surmount the precision short of a length delivery that has been the logical professional bowler's reply to this attempt to 'process' him out of the game.

PETER WALKER on why covered wickets had not improved stroke-making.

AFTER I've retired they should open the pitches to the elements.

PETER ROEBUCK, Somerset batsman, **1985**.

IF they want pitches that do absolutely bugger all, that's easy. If they want pitches that are dangerous, that's easy too. Good cricket pitches, the sort we think we produce more often than not, are difficult. The dividing line between a flat pitch and a dodgy one is very thin, and occasionally you miscalculate. If the TCCB aren't careful, they will frighten groundsmen into being responsible for producing exactly the sort of cricket they used to moan about before.

RON ALLSOPP, Trent Bridge groundsman, **1988**.

SHORT boundaries, by decreasing the opportunities for good fielding, rob cricket of half its charm.

WISDEN editorial, **1906**.

I can hear you my lord, but where are you?

JOHN NEWMAN (Hampshire) joining his captain, Lionel Tennyson, at the wicket in bad light.

You can see the moon. How far do you want to see?

ARTHUR JEPSON, umpire, turning down appeal for bad light by Jack Bond in Gillette Cup tie, Lancashire *v* Gloucestershire at Old Trafford, **1971** (the match finished at 8.50 p.m.).

IF I can see 'em, I can hit 'em.

DAVID HUGHES, before scoring 24 off one over to decide the above tie.

I'VE come out here to develop a few photographs.

FRANK WORRELL to Godfrey Evans, England's wicket-keeper, in murky light at Trent Bridge in **1957**. Worrell, who made 191 in the West Indies' first innings, had been on the field for more than 20 hours, yet still opened when his side followed on.

THERE is an accent on sameness in approach, sameness in method, none of which helps to make the game more eye-catching. This uniformity has extended itself into wearing apparel – a coloured cap is looked upon as definitely 'Non-U' among professionals – and in batting styles. Numbers one to eight are carbon copies of each other both in technique and tactical approach.

PETER WALKER in *The Cricketer*, **1963**.

> There was a young fresher called Jessop
> Who was pitching 'em less up and less up,
> 'Til one of the pros
> Got a blow on the nose
> And said: 'In a helmet I'll dress up'.

CAMBRIDGE UNIVERSITY LIMERICK making early reference to use of batting helmets, after Gilbert Jessop bowled bumpers, Varsity Match, **1896**.

IF someone had produced a batting helmet during the Bodyline series, I would certainly have worn it.

SIR DONALD BRADMAN.

I don't know what the game's coming to. You wouldn't get me wearing one of those plastic things.

BRIAN CLOSE, on Tony Cordle's use of a fielding helmet for Glamorgan, following near-fatal injury to his team-mate Roger Davis, **1971**.

THE increased weights of bats has contributed to our weakness in hooking. The shot demands speed of stroke and timing. How much simpler it is to swat a fly with a rolled up newspaper than with a telephone directory.

DENIS COMPTON in *Cricket and All That*, **1978**.

I wore a shilling cap, a sixpenny belt with a snake-clasp and brown boots. At the trial I bowled in my sweater, but I was better off than Arthur Mold of Lancashire, who couldn't take his off because he had no shirt on underneath. My shirt was blue, but I got a white one with my first money.

GEORGE HIRST on his trial for Yorkshire, **1889**.

I only wish some of the players' trousers fitted better.

THE DUKE OF EDINBURGH when asked if he had any complaints about modern cricket in **1987**.

IT is a good thing to carry a scarf to put round the neck between innings. It looks smart – and there is no harm in doing your side credit – and cools one off gradually.

CROSS-ARROW, *The Cricketer*, **1927**.

IF you like a white sun hat always carry one with you. C. B. Fry played some of his greatest innings in a sun hat.

CROSS-ARROW, *The Cricketer*, **1927**.

I'M going to make them wear their caps this season. After all, you don't get awarded your county floppy hat, do you?

JACK BOND, Lancashire CCC manager, **1985**.

PLAYERS will not be allowed on the field with coloured tams or hats, long plaited hair or dreadlocks.

RULES of Leeward Islands Cricket Association, to discriminate against Rasta-farians. Introduced when Victor Eddy, last Rasta in first-class cricket, represented Leewards in **1970s**.

WHEN I see a young man who has an expensive and pretty hair-do, I have doubts as to his ability to reach Test standard.

TED DEXTER in *A Walk to the Wicket*, **1985**.

WE had different ideas of fitness. To me the best preparation for batting, bowling and fielding was batting, bowling and fielding. I doubt if many of my contemporaries, especially the older ones, did many exercises. I have often tried to picture Evans and Compton doing press-ups in the outfield before the day's play but so far have failed miserably.

PETER MAY, chairman of Test selectors, in *A Game Enjoyed*, **1985**.

IF I want to get fit for bowling, I do a lot of bowling.

BRIAN STATHAM, Lancashire and England, **1974**.

I'M resigned to the fact that I may end up in a wheelchair any time.

GRAHAM DILLEY, Kent pace bowler, returning after neck operation, **1985**.

DURING the winter I train on 20 fags and a couple of pints of lager and a prolonged diet of cricket talk.

BRIAN BRAIN, Gloucestershire seamer, *Another Day, Another Match*, **1981**.

A fag, a cough, a cup of coffee.

BRIAN STATHAM, England pace bowler, on a pre-match breakfast. (Source: *The Test Within*, Frank Tyson, **1987**.)

I absolutely insist that all my boys should be in bed before breakfast.

COLIN INGLEBY-MACKENZIE, explaining the reason for Hampshire's success under his captaincy, on BBC Radio, **1960s**.

IT just goes to show the difference a few hours' extra sleep can make.

GRAHAM DILLEY, tongue in cheek, after taking five for 55 *v* West Indies at Lord's, **1988**. A curfew had been imposed following the antics in the First Test which cost Gatting the captaincy.

I go to a party on Friday night, sometimes until 4 a.m., then score 50 and take five wickets.

OMAR HENRY on becoming the first coloured player to play for South Africa, **1987**.

IF these young men think they can field all day, on such a day as Thursday was, dance all night at the Hawks ball (which they were practically compelled to attend) and then do themselves justice with the bat the next morning, then they are very much mistaken.

'CANTAB' on Cambridge University cricket in *The Cricketer*, **1925**.

SLEEP is essential, especially during the cricket season; we would place eight hours as an absolute minimum; ten is better still. Smoking is bad, especially cigarettes, and, of course, excess in eating and drinking is still worse. Reading late at night, too, spells ruin for the eyes.

D. J. KNIGHT's first axiom of batsmanship – good health.

VEGETARIANISM may be a cure for all the ills which flesh is heir to, but it is wretched stuff to make runs on. For the whole month of May I could get neither runs nor wickets.

G. L. JESSOP on his poor form in May **1898**, after an attack of renal colic.

THE 'Old Man' [W.G.] was much concerned over my ill success, and resolved to prescribe for me in his own fashion. I forget whether it was Goelet 1889, or Moët 1886 . . . anyway it had the desired effect, and I bade farewell to vegetarianism for ever.

G. L. JESSOP on his return to form.

HEY, Greigy. This champagne's all right, but the blackcurrant jam tastes of fish.

DEREK RANDALL, sampling caviar on MCC tour to India, **1976/7**.

But, beggin' your lordships' pardons, it strikes me as bein' like this, beggin' your lordships' pardons – if Ah can go down to Lord's and get drunk and mek a century 'fore lunch, then Ah thinks it ud pay t'Notts Committee to get mi drunk afore every match.

BILLY BARNES, reprimanded by Nottinghamshire committee after arriving late and drunk – but still scoring a century against Middlesex at Lord's. (From Neville Cardus's *Autobiography*, **1947**.)

Kids in the West feel a bit peckish and buy a carton of junk-food. Plenty here can't afford to do that. So they have to eat lots of fruit and other good wholesome grub that happens to be the cheapest and the best for them. Add all the bits and pieces together and you get a long, long queue of fit, lean, loose-moving youngsters who are superbly fitted to the job.

ARTHUR WAIGHT, West Indies physio, explaining the West Indies' surfeit of fast bowlers in the **1980s**.

We used to eat so many salads, there was a danger of contracting myxomatosis.

RAY EAST, describing lunchtime offerings on the county circuit, in *A Funny Turn*, **1983**.

You can't consider yourself a county cricketer until you've eaten a ton and a half of lettuce.

GARY SOBERS welcoming West Indian newcomer to the circuit.

I always have my lunch at 1.30 p.m.

GEORGE GUNN, Nottinghamshire batsman, deliberately giving his wicket away after learning lunch interval was later than usual.

I always feel better after my luncheon.

W. G. GRACE, when asked by A. C. MacLaren if he ever felt nervous. (Related by MacLaren, BBC Home Service, **1935**.)

THOROUGH sportsmen they were and men who made a day of a match on Saturday. Where we went to play, there we dined. Not like the present club cricket: 'When is the next train home?'

S. M. J. WOODS (Somerset, England), comparing club cricket in the 1890s and **1923**.

THERE is a lot of cricket spirit and cricket philosophy in that statement 'where we played, there we dined'.

LAURENCE WOODHOUSE, 'Ruminations' in *The Cricketer*, **1923**.

MOST county cricketers play the game for the life rather than the living. For them it's the motorways of England rather than the jet lanes of the world. It's sausage, egg and chips at Watford Gap rather than *vol-au-vent* and small talk on the Governor-General's lawns in Barbados.

MICHAEL CAREY.

THE domestic treadmill of cricket is in need of an overhaul. The fixture lists are beginning to read like a British Rail handbook, with players running from one connection to the next.

SIMON JONES, legal adviser to the Keep Sunday Special Campaign, article in *The Cricketer*, **1988**.

I could a bowt t'taxi for less.

ARTHUR WOOD. Yorkshire wicket-keeper, after rushing by taxi from Scarborough for his Test debut *v* Australians at Lord's, **1938**.

A whole generation of professional cricketers has emerged who don't know the sheer pleasure of lazing around on a free Sunday . . . the Saturday nights when you didn't have to climb into the car and drive 150 miles after a long day in the field. You could have a few pints with the opposition, a night on the town and then relax next morning in bed with the Sunday papers, contemplating nothing more strenuous than a game of golf in the afternoon.

BRIAN BRAIN, *Another Day, Another Match*, **1981**.

THERE was nothing else to do but drink. I saw so many balls I couldn't miss.

FRANK WORRELL after his double hundred in Kanpur, West Indies' tour of India, **1952/3**.

THE wheels of the social bandwagon have come off. The five cans of ale that the old-timers might have enjoyed before a civilised dinner each night have turned into prolonged, boredom drinking in public.

BOB WILLIS, *Lasting the Pace*, **1985**.

THE hardest drug anyone would have taken would have been Valium, and that would have been on sleepless nights.

IAN BOTHAM, as the allegations of drug-taking on tour began to appear, **1984**.

I'M aware he smokes dope, but doesn't everyone?

TIM HUDSON on Ian Botham, **1986**. The comments led to his sacking as Botham's agent.

BOTHAM: I *did* smoke pot.

MAIL ON SUNDAY headline, **1986**.

I have been to many functions where some of the great cricketers of the past have been present. . . . To see some of them sink their drink is to witness performances as awe-inspiring as ever any of them displayed on the cricket field.

IAN BOTHAM, excusing use of marijuana, **1986**.

CERTAINLY I am told you can play cricket better after a marijuana cigarette than after a couple of pints of beer.

LORD WIGODER, Old Bailey judge and cricket follower.

IN international cricket a player should be made to fight for everything he gets on the field in gratitude for all the things he gets for nothing off the field.

ARTHUR MAILEY.

BEHIND the façade of the Test class player and the glamour attributed to the international game by the press, lies Mr Average county cricketer. No £500 appearance money for a series against the tourists, no overseas tours with their opportunities to broaden one's outlook and, outside of their local papers, little publicity. For most, intermixed with the outdoor life and grand fellowship that exists among the 17 counties, lies a lot of heartache, fierce disappointments, sudden elations and regular separations from their families.

PETER WALKER.

SOMETIMES I'm standing in the slips and I start day dreaming. I think, what the hell am I doing here? What a waste of time. There must be more important things to do for a living. And sitting in the pavilion after I've been in, that's the worst of the lot. I can't stand watching cricket.

BARRY RICHARDS, **1974**.

IT has been suggested tonight that no one may again do what I've been lucky enough to do this season. I don't know about that but I do know this – if he does, he'll be tired.

GEORGE HIRST, after scoring over 2000 runs and taking more than 200 wickets for Yorkshire in a season, **1906**.

IF anyone beats it, they'll be bloody tired.

FRED TRUEMAN, on becoming England's leading Test wicket-taker, **1964**.

WHEN Fred reached his 307 he said afterwards that anyone who passed him would be very tired. Well, you can tell him I'm not.

BOB WILLIS, on becoming England's leading Test wicket-taker in New Zealand, **1984**.

ALL the time I keep telling myself and telling the others, 'It could be worse, fellas. We could be putting a helmet on for a shift down t'pit.'

GEOFF BOYCOTT on bad days.

THIS miners' strike is ridiculous. There's tea ladies at the top of the mine who are earning more than county cricketers. Arthur Scargill ought to come down here and try bowling twenty overs.

RAY ILLINGWORTH, then Leicestershire captain, **1975**.

THERE'S no pressure in Yorkshire cricket. My mate gets up at half-past four every morning to go down t'pit. That's what you call pressure.

STEVE OLDHAM, on his appointment as Yorkshire cricket manager, **1989**.

I'M going to threaten them with going back down the pit.

LES TAYLOR to his Leicestershire fast-bowling colleague Jon Agnew who had threatened to take up a broadcasting career if he was not picked for England, **1988**.

I'VE got six CSEs, and this has to be a better opportunity than hoping for a job with the water authority.

MARTIN CHARTERS, 16, waiting to hear if he had been accepted for the first cricket YTS programme, **1988**.

THEY wanted me to be a bloody doorman.

NORMAN COWANS, leaving club side in Brisbane because they could not find him suitable employment, **1986**.

IT is a contrasting sign of the times that the star player is making so much money indirectly from the game that created him that unless Auntie Clara and the two poodles are allowed to tour with him, he is not disposed to represent England overseas.

WILFRED WOOLLER, referring to Lock's statement that he would not be available for the **1962/3** tour of Australia unless his wife went too.

I don't care what money I get man – it's the buzz of playing for Australia that's got me.

GREG MATTHEWS, making Test debut, **1983**.

BRIGHTER cricket, more entertaining cricket, quicker cricket, less cricket had its variant of support. But my belief is that whatever cricket reforms were instigated, they will prove no lasting panacea for financial illness . . . first-class cricket will stand or fall in this decade by business foresight and planning.

WILFRED WOOLLER, **1961**.

IT should surprise no-one that cricket is not self-supporting. It never has been.

COLIN COWDREY in *MCC*, **1976**.

CRICKET must be the only business where you can make more money in one day than you can in three.

PAT GIBSON, *Daily Express*, **1975**.

THE modern cricketer will do a lot for money. He will hawk autographed miniature cricket bats in Calcutta, one of the world's most impoverished cities, to children in the crowd at £15 a time.

JOHN WOODCOCK, *The Times*, **1977**.

WHEN it comes to a contract, loyalty doesn't count for much.

ANDREW KENNEDY, cricket coach at Taunton School, when one of his pupils signed for Middlesex after getting three years' coaching by Somerset.

MR Stoddart, Mr Woods, will you please have a drink with me. I think I have enough money to pay out of my benefit.

WILLIAM BARNES (Nottinghamshire, England) after a poorly attended benefit match.

BARNES be paid 7s 6d for batting when his score reaches 50, and also 10s 6d per match for bowling when he captures six wickets per match, not unless.

SYDNEY BARNES'S contract with Rishton, **1896**.

CRICKET in London is nearly all professional; even the gentlemen make a profession of it.

REV. JAMES PYCROFT, **1851**.

ONE well-known cricketer in particular . . . has made larger profits by playing cricket than any professional ever made.

SHAMATEURISM, as noted in case of W. G. Grace in *Lillywhite's Cricketers' Companion*, **1878**.

THROUGH the spontaneous generosity of some road sweepers, who apparently rested from their labours for a short while, I was presented with a collection of 1s 5½d.

D. L. A. JEPHSON on scoring 200 for Ashley *v* Hornsey in **1903**. He had refused to play for Gentlemen *v* Players in order to play in the club match.

I proved that I do possess the dedication and determination to build a big innings. I've always got out after about 160 for Northants before. This time I wanted to see if I was able to hold on. I must admit the financial incentives also played a part.

ALLAN LAMB on his 294 for Orange Free State, a South African record. The runs earned him around £26,500 in sponsors' awards.

WHILST recognising that the Amateurs were fully entitled to the repayment of genuine out-of-pocket expenses incurred while playing, and that the counties themselves must be the final judge of such claims, the committee were disturbed by the apparent over-liberal interpretation of the words 'expenses' in certain cases that had come to their notice.

REPORT of special MCC committee, chaired by the Duke of Norfolk, on amateur status, **1958**.

STEADY, Mr Christopherson, steady! I'm getting ten bob a run.

TED PEATE to Stanley Christopherson, his last-wicket partner, during England v
Australia Test series, **1884**.

THE captain's orders had to come before Teddy Peate's ten bobs,
and I was caught off a mishit next over. Peate was quite sad about it.

CHRISTOPHERSON'S account of the above incident.

IN all games where there is any pecuniary benefit to be derived, the
professional invariably beats the amateur, and the reason is easily
found in the fact that the professional works much harder than the
amateur.

F. R. SPOFFORTH in *Great Bowlers* (eds G. W. Beldham and C. B. Fry), **1906**.

THERE must always be a limit to the number of professionals for
whom room can be found in one county eleven.

SYDNEY PARDON, editor, *Wisden*, **1897**.

THE end of the 1961 season has brought forth from the leading
critics their annual plea for more amateurs in the game and a
consequently brighter approach. They are forgetting that the game
is played by a majority of professional players and that the
contemporary amateur is usually as much of an employee of a
county as any professional. As for an 'amateur approach', a careful
study will reveal that this too is a modern myth. Today's alleged
leaders in brighter cricket are often the dullest and most cautious
members of their sides.

PETER WALKER, **1961**.

PRAY God no professional may ever captain England.

LORD HAWKE.

AMATEURS always have made, and always will make, the best
captains; and this is only natural.

A. G. STEEL.

T. Emmett be made captain in the absence of a gentleman.

YORKSHIRE COMMITTEE MINUTES, **1878**.

I'M very glad we have an amateur again.

MIDDLESEX COMMITTEE MAN, mistakenly, to Mike Brearley on his appointment as county captain, **1971**.

AMES, I see you are wearing the county tie there. You know, don't you, that strictly speaking you are not entitled to wear it . . . I think it would be better if you didn't in future.

KENT OFFICIAL to Les Ames, professional, **1930s**. (From *The Gloves Are Off*, Godfrey Evans, **1960**.)

I shave twice a day so you can shave once.

LORD HAWKE to his Yorkshire professionals after assuming captaincy, **1883**.

I have heard some English captains speak to their professionals like dogs.

JOE DARLING, Australian captain, **1902**.

IT is rather curious that the Australians themselves do not realise that our professionals prefer to be 'on their own' off the field rather than to be in the same hotel as the amateurs. Indeed, I know that some of our professionals would prefer to have second-class passages on board ship rather than having to dress each night for dinner.

LORD HAWKE.

THE average professional cricketer is purely and simply a trades-man, and in most cases he has learnt his trade in a pretty grim school. He has a six-day-a-week job, and the regularity of his work is likely to drive him into a groove. Unless he is a very exceptional man he stays in that groove for security and the result is loss of incentive, the spirit of adventure and enterprise.

ARTHUR MAILEY.

No games have given me more pleasure than these tussles with the professors.

G. L. JESSOP on the Gentlemen *v* Players matches.

THE plain-spoken little bumpkin, in his eagerness and delight, and forgetting the style in which we were always accustomed to impress our aristocratical playmates with our acknowledgement of their rank and station, bawled out – 'Ah! it was *tedious* near you, Sir!' The familiarity of his tone, and the genuine Hampshire dialect in which it was spoken, set the whole ground laughing.

JOHN NYREN, *The Young Cricketer's Tutor* on Lambert, 'The Little Farmer', almost bowling the Duke of Dorset with an off-break.

HIGH and low, rich and poor, greet one another practically on an equality, and sad will be the day for England if Socialism ever succeeds in putting class v class and thus ending sports which have made England.

LORD HAWKE, *Recollections and Reminiscences*, **1924**.

BOLSHEVISM is rampant, and seeks to abolish all laws and rules, and this year cricket has not escaped its attack.

LORD HARRIS in *The Cricketer*, **1922**. Hammond chose to play for Gloucestershire rather than his native Kent.

BUT the second day was played under the cloud of the General Strike, and since then serious cricket at Oxford has been seen no more. Legge, after covering incredible distances at illegal speeds in his Vauxhall, transporting workers, ended up by driving a 'bus in London; Holmes, Stephenson and Abell joined the constabulary; Richardson, Greenstock, Surrurier and McCanlis have been acting as dockers at Bristol, Hull and Liverpool.

'ISIS' on Oxford cricket during the General Strike, in *The Cricketer*, **1926**.

THE single most important change has been the decline of the personality player and the rise of the professional attitude . . . it is a product of the times, a tangent from Trade Unionism.

COLIN COWDREY in *MCC*, **1976**.

No country which has cricket as one of its national games has yet gone Communist. On this I found my trust that the new regime in West Indian Grenada will turn out to be not so extreme Left-Wing as predicted.

WOODROW WYATT in the *Sunday Mirror*, **1979**.

CRICKET is certainly among the most powerful links which keep our Empire together. It is one of the greatest contributions which the British people have made to the cause of humanity.

RANJITSINHJI.

CRICKET has done more to consolidate the Empire than any other influence.

LORD HARRIS, *A Few Short Runs*, **1921**.

ON the cricket grounds of the Empire is fostered the spirit of never knowing when you are beaten, of playing for your side and not for yourself, and of never giving up a game as lost . . . the future of cricket and the Empire is so inseparably connected.

LORD HAWKE, in introduction to Warner's *Imperial Cricket*.

SAY that cricket has nothing to do with politics and you say that cricket has nothing to do with life.

JOHN ARLOTT.

YOU think my run-up was long. You should hear my speeches.

WES HALL, now a Barbados Senator, **1987**.

DID you see that, sir? That means war!

MCC member to colleague at Lord's when a green baize cloth was placed over one of the Long Room busts, **1939**,

My successes with the Army are owing in a great measure to the manly sports of Great Britain, and one sport above all – cricket.

ASCRIBED to a Duke of Wellington speech in the Lords by Arthur Haygarth. (Quoted by G. D. Martineau, *The Cricketer*, **1959**, who admits he has been unable to find the source.)

A sportsman is like a soldier who is always ready to help the country.

GENERAL ZIA of Pakistan persuading Imran to come out of retirement, **1988**.

I am always ready to serve the nation and the game.

IMRAN, acquiescing, **1988**.

YOUNG ensigns and lieutenants, who had never seen a battle before, rushed to meet death as though they had been playing cricket.

DUKE OF WELLINGTON on the Battle of Waterloo.

I don't wonder at the courage of you English when you teach your children to play with cannon-balls.

CZAR NICHOLAS I watching a cricket match at Chatham.

DURING the afternoon heavy aerial fighting developed between our fighters and the German bombers, and the sirens went. The boys were anxious to continue play, but there was just an outside chance of one being hit, so we sent them to the nearby shelters. I regret to record that the Forty Club repaired to the bar.

HENRY GRIERSON, founder and Honorary Secretary of the Forty Club, on their match *v* Public Schools at Richmond, August **1940**.

A visit to Lord's on a dark December day was a sobering experience; there were sandbags everywhere, and the Long Room was stripped and bare, with its treasures safely stored beneath ground, but the turf was a wondrous green, old Time on the Grand Stand was gazing serenely at the nearest balloon, and one felt that somehow it would take more than totalitarian war to put an end to cricket.

MAJOR H. S. ALTHAM, *Wisden*, **1940**.

FIELD-MARSHAL ROMMEL . . . would have made a great cricket captain if his birthplace had been slightly different.

IAN PEEBLES.

IF we had shown that kind of attitude and guts during the war that our cricketers have in the West Indies, Hitler would have walked over us.

BRIAN CLOSE, **1986**.

SAY, when do they begin?

GROUCHO MARX, watching Middlesex bat at Lord's, **1960s**.

I don't think I can be expected to take seriously a game which takes less than three days to reach its conclusion.

TOM STOPPARD, playwright and cricket buff, on baseball in New York, **1984**.

THERE is nothing wrong with the game but only with the players' approach to it; unless this is remedied soon, most players will have lost the ability, through lack of practice, to play strokes, and the game will face an age of strokeless batsmen opposed by throwers and draggers – a complete prostitution of the art of cricket.

WARWICKSHIRE REPORT, after attendances fell by more than half a million in a single year, **1959**.

FIRST-class cricket is a subtle as well as a strenuous game. It is a thing of leisure, albeit of leisure today not easily found or arranged; a three-act play, not a slapstick turn.

R. C. ROBERTSON-GLASGOW, *Wisden*, **1945**.

I'M told that it was not until the first week of June 1946 that the public was told that county cricket was dying, and of course the game has been on its last legs ever since.

DOUG INSOLE, *Cricket from the Middle*, **1960**.

CRICKETERS do not expect anyone to watch three-day games.

PETER ROEBUCK, Somerset batsman, **1985**.

EVERYONE, without exception, approved the cricketing argument.

AC SMITH, TCCB chief executive, at the **1989** winter meeting, supporting a total switch to four-day championship cricket.

THERE is massive opposition to this scheme among those who pay to watch the game. Championship cricket is more than just a breeding ground for Test players.

TONY VANN, Yorkshire committee man, attempting to rally grass-roots opposition to four-day cricket, **1989**.

IT would have been a paltry and unworthy thing to deprive Australia, by means of a money bribe, of her finest batsman.

WISDEN on efforts to attract Victor Trumper, Australian, into English county cricket, **1908**.

THEY should stop whining about overseas players. There are too many old men in English cricket. Look at Ray Illingworth, at the age of 50, Geoff Boycott and so many others like them – these are the men who are stopping the young players coming through.

ASIF IQBAL on moves to reduce the number of overseas players, **1983**.

WITHOUT overseas players, the English county game would be dead.

RICHARD HADLEE, *At the Double*, **1985**.

IF it is true that overseas players are keeping English players out in the counties, then Yorkshire should have supplied the bulk of the English Test team.

IMRAN KHAN, *All Round View*, **1988**.

ARGUMENTS are put forward in favour of transforming the great game into a thing of immense rapidity – a sort of Bolshevist cricket devoted to hurricane yorkers and 'swipes'. This, of course, would make quite impossible the science, the law and beauty which are the charm of cricket – to cricketers.

GUARDIAN leader, **1918**. The end of wartime had brought calls to liven up cricket.

IN real cricket, the player who has developed imagination and skill makes the game, but in the one-day match it is the other way round. The match dictates to the player.

BRIAN CLOSE, prior to his sacking by Yorkshire, **1970**.

THROW down some sawdust, everybody put on top hats and red noses, and you've got the John Player League.

BRIAN CLOSE, **1969**.

FOR six days, thou shalt push up and down the line but on the seventh day thou shalt swipe.

DOUG PADGETT, Yorkshire batsman, offering 11th commandment on the advent of Sunday League, **1969**.

To a man of my age the introduction of the Sunday League has been nothing less than an act of cruelty.

TOM GRAVENEY, England and Worcestershire batsman, **1970**.

I can hardly remember an innings I have played in one-day cricket.

GREG CHAPPELL, **1984**.

THERE is a possibility that your ability as a player may well be analysed by future generations on your one-day statistics. That's the day I dread most.

ALLAN BORDER, Australian captain, **1985**.

ONE-day cricket is like fast food. Nobody wants to cook.

VIV RICHARDS, West Indies captain, after tour of India, **1988**.

ONE-day cricket has killed outswing. Bowlers have got to come wide of the wicket and arrow the ball towards the leg side. They open up their bodies and become arm bowlers.

RICHARD HADLEE in *At the Double*, **1985**.

SIXTEEN needed from two overs. If we win, jubilation; if not, despair. It matters not how we played the game, but whether we won or lost.

VIC MARKS on Sunday League cricket, **1988**.

THERE was a time, about ten years ago, when I was unable to devour my roast beef and Yorkshire pudding, such was the tension engendered by the prospect of a Sunday League game. Somerset were invariably in contention for the title, the little county ground at Taunton would be crammed with vociferous spectators and a life-and-death struggle would ensue. In those days I was rarely called on to bowl, and sometimes we would win so comfortably that I did not have to bat either, but I would finish the day completely exhausted. Today my plate will be emptied. A combination of old age, dwindling crowds and a familiarity with the Sunday pattern has restored my appetite.

VIC MARKS, Somerset vice-captain, **1988**.

THIS game is injecting a dementia into the souls of those who play it.

BILL O'REILLY, *Sydney Morning Herald*, on effects of one-day cricket, **1982**.

IT is surely the loveliest scene in England and the most disarming sound. From the ranks of the unseen dead for ever passing along our country lanes, the Englishman falls out for a moment to look over the gate of the cricket field and smile.

SIR JAMES BARRIE.

WE all started playing somewhere like this, and this is where we should all finish; back in village cricket that gave us our start.

EDDIE PAYNTER (Lancashire, England), then 58, on playing for Ingrow *v* Denholme.

THERE is no other game at which the confirmed duffer is so persistent and so undepressed.

E. V. LUCAS, *English Leaves*.

THE greatest duffer at the game is the most enthusiastic.

R. A. FITZGERALD, MCC secretary, 1863–1876.

HAS Tate bowled you with a fast off-break, third ball, before your eye was set? Come and be bowled first ball by Mr Muggridge, with a fast shooter, before you have taken guard. Then, indeed, you are a cricketer.

R. C. ROBERTSON-GLASGOW on village cricket.

OUR lbw rule . . . is plain. One end you are out, even if struck on the head; the other end you are in, till you are bowled (undeniably) or caught (far from the ground). We admire this system, and are jealous of our traditions.

R. C. ROBERTSON-GLASGOW.

VILLAGERS do not think village cricket is funny.

JOHN ARLOTT, Foreword to Gerald Howat's *Village Cricket*, **1981**.

THE trouble with school sides is that they are run by schoolteachers and selected by schoolteachers. Coaches would pick different sides. You learn so much more from one Second XI game than from umpteen school games.

PIRAN HOLLOWAY, Taunton schoolboy and Warwickshire wicket-keeper in **1988**.

6

Philosophers All

Cricket Thoughts and Theories

WHAT do they know of cricket who only cricket know?

C. L. R. JAMES, *Beyond a Boundary*, **1963**.

IF there is any game in the world that attracts the half-baked theorists more than cricket I have yet to hear of it.

FRED TRUEMAN, *Fred Trueman's Book of Cricket*, **1964**.

CRICKET more than any other game is inclined towards sentimentalism and cant.

SIR NEVILLE CARDUS, *A Fourth Innings with Cardus*, **1981**.

WHAT is human life but a game of cricket?

THE DUKE OF DORSET, **1777**.

THERE is no crisis in cricket, there is only the next ball.

W. G. GRACE.

THEY say onlookers see most of the game. But not always. The batsman at the other end sees more.

M. A. NOBLE.

WHAT'S the good of me going in? If I miss 'em I'm out and if I hit 'em I'm out. Let's start the next innings.

> W. BUTTRESS (Cambridgeshire, **1860s**), one of nature's No. 11s, on being found up a tree when it was his turn to bat.

YOU must treat a new cricket ball like a new bride.

> MICKY STEWART giving advice to bowlers, **1986**.

LOOK what the silly buggers have done now. Cost the club another 13s 6d.

> JIM SMITH, taking the new ball to end a stubborn tenth-wicket stand, Nottinghamshire *v* Middlesex, **1938**.

I haven't done it right often.

> JIM LAKER, asked if his eight wickets for two runs for England against The Rest was his best-bowling analysis, Park Avenue, **1950**.

IF those artifical pitches had stayed down they would have given a tremendous fillip to the development of similar pitches at grassroots level.

> FREDDIE BROWN, National Cricket Association president, regretting the removal of certain synthetic pitches, **1984**.

A cricketer – a creature very nearly as stupid as a dog.

> BERNARD LEVIN, *Times* columnist, **1965**.

NOBODY'S perfect. You know what happened to the last man who was – they crucified him.

> GEOFFREY BOYCOTT, answering criticism of his rate of scoring, **1979**.

IF I knew I was going to die today I'd still want to hear the cricket scores.

> J. H. HARDY.

WELL, I shan't be here next year but I'd like to be buried in the middle there to make a good bumpy pitch for our bowlers.

CHARLES CUNLIFFE, Kent slow bowler, dying of consumption during Canterbury Week, **1881**.

YOU must remember, man, one beautiful day doesn't make a summer.

VIV RICHARDS after West Indies' defeat by Pakistan.

I can remember some good Saturdays against the West Indies before – the only trouble is that the Thursdays, Fridays, Mondays and Tuesdays were a bit of a disaster.

JOHN EMBUREY refusing to get carried away after a successful first day under his leadership in the Second Test v West Indies in **1988**. His caution proved justified.

CRICKET is a situation game. When the situation is dead, the game is dead.

TREVOR BAILEY.

IF we win the toss you will wish we had been a bit later still.

W. G. GRACE to a very angry Lord Harris when Grace's team arrived late at Canterbury because of a train hold-up, **1883**. Grace did win the toss.

THE game of cricket, philosophically considered, is a standing panegyric on the English character: none but an orderly and sensible race of people would so amuse themselves.

REV. JAMES PYCROFT, *The Cricket Field*, **1851**.

PRIVATE enterprise in cricket might not be regarded as the last word, and ultimate State direction would not do it any harm.

MANNY SHINWELL, Labour MP, after another poor English summer, **1950**.

WE play the game and, if we lose, we should go out because we are a civilised people.

SRI LANKAN, aged 84, voting in country's **1988** election despite threat of unrest and civil war.

CRICKET can be a bridge and a glue. . . . Cricket for peace is my mission.

PRESISENT ZIA of Pakistan, on a goodwill visit to India during Test series between the two countries, **1987**.

CRICKET? It civilises people and creates good gentlemen. I want everyone to play cricket in Zimbabwe. I want ours to be a nation of gentlemen.

ROBERT MUGABE, Prime Minister of Zimbabwe, **1984**.

THE Conservatives played like England cricketers – too many rash strokes and run-outs, dropped catches and bowling anywhere but the stumps.

NORMAN TEBBIT in the wake of Tories' defeat in Euro elections, **1989**.

CRICKET shouldn't be used as a political football.

DAVID GRAVENEY, Gloucestershire captain.

THE public need to be educated up to cricket.

ROY KILNER, Yorkshire cricketer.

COMPREHENSIVES don't produce cricketers.

JIM LAKER.

BAD luck, sir, you were just getting settled in.

FRED TRUEMAN to Oxbridge batsman. After a long loosening-up exercise, the unfortunate batsman had been bowled for nought, first ball.

To go to a cricket match for nothing but cricket is as though a man were to go into an inn for nothing but drink.

NEVILLE CARDUS, *Autobiography*, **1947**.

THERE'S more ways of getting out than is shown in t'rules.

WILFRED RHODES, **1930**.

You don't get good players out by sledging.

IMRAN KHAN, *All Round View*, **1988**.

THE first consideration is the mental outlook of the individual who can, if he chooses, soil any game by his interpretation of its character.

DON BRADMAN, *Wisden*, **1939**.

THE most famous cricketers are too big to play county cricket.

IAN BOTHAM.

IT's a different game now but people won't accept it. . . . Trueman would still be a good bowler but he wouldn't be called Fiery Fred.

IAN BOTHAM in *It Sort of Clicks*, Botham and Peter Roebuck, **1986**.

THE older I get, the better a cricketer I seem to become.

JIM LAKER, *Cricket Contrasts*, **1985**.

TOO many people in cricket live in the past.

IAN BOTHAM.

HOBBS, Hammond and Broad: it doesn't quite ring true, does it?

CHRIS BROAD on becoming the third Englishman to score centuries in three successive Tests in a series in Australia, **1986**.

IT may not be cricket, but it's four.

> E. M. GRACE pulling a ball from outside off-stump, which was considered unethical in the mid nineteenth century.

KEEP the left shoulder well forward and say your prayers.

> A. N. HORNBY'S precept for a cricketing life to the nine-year-old A. C. MacLaren.

IN regard to the matter of praying, I expect those who do not use their left shoulder make up in prayer what they lack in shoulder work.

> A. C. MACLAREN inveighing against the two-eyed stance, 1921.

ENGLISH cricket, for as long as I can remember, has been bedevilled by the cult of the left elbow.

> LORD COBHAM, former MCC president, 1967.

I realised just in time that unless I put bat to ball, I'd have to change in another dressing room.

> GLENN TURNER, 1983.

I think I know what that 'B' on your cap stands for.

> JOHN DANIELL, Somerset captain, to opposing batsman who had spent four hours accumulating 50.

I play best when I'm surrounded by people who appreciate me.

> GEOFFREY BOYCOTT, 1980.

IT's not comforting to feel I will no longer be a power in the land. I have found personal success very gratifying. I think it's going to be hard for me to drop out of it all.

> JACK HOBBS, retiring from Test cricket, BBC Radio, 1930.

WHEN I walk off a cricket ground for the last time – whenever that will be – it will be with an enormous sense of relief.

BARRY RICHARDS, **1978**.

WHO ever hoped like a cricketer?

R. C. ROBERTSON-GLASGOW, *Cricket Prints*, **1943**.

I regularly wanted to lock myself in the toilet if I got out. I wanted to be alone.

GLENN TURNER, Worcestershire and New Zealand batsman, **1970**.

YOU should play every game as if it's your last, but make sure you perform well enough to make sure it's not.

JOHN EMBUREY'S philosophical reflections on becoming Gatting's successor as captain, **1988**.

I'LL be telling them to do better than I did.

GRAHAM GOOCH'S advice to the debutants in his side for the Fifth Test *v* West Indies, **1988**. Gooch made a 'pair' on his own Test debut.

PEOPLE no longer ask me if he advises me, because it's obvious he doesn't . . . or if he does, that I'm taking no notice!

CHRIS COWDREY, on comparisons with his father.

YOU lead in May, and I shall catch you in June.

PHILIP MEAD to Hampshire team-mates having pre-season nets.

THERE was no triumph in me as I watched the receding figure. I felt like a boy who had killed a dove.

ARTHUR MAILEY on bowling his idol Victor Trumper in a Grade match in Sydney (Redfern *v* Paddington).

I used to bowl tripe, then I wrote it, now I sell it.

NOTICE above Arthur Mailey's butcher's shop near Sydney.

MY word, I know what all the problems are. I've failed at everything.

JOHN ARLOTT, asked whether playing first-class cricket would have been an advantage in his job, farewell broadcast, BBC Radio, **1980**.

I can see I'm going to have to do a lot of bowling if I play for this side. I think I'd better cut my run down.

'BOMBER' WELLS, who bowled off three paces, after debut for Gloucestershire at Bristol.

I can bowl so slow that if I don't like a ball I can run after it and bring it back.

J. M. BARRIE, **1926**. (From Neville Cardus's *Autobiography*, 1947.)

WHEN you're an off-spinner there's not much point glaring at a batsman. If I glared at Viv Richards he'd just hit me even further.

DAVID ACFIELD, Essex, **1982**.

NEVER mind, I've got a little kid at home who will make it up for me.

'POOR FRED' TATE, after dropping the catch that lost England the Old Trafford Test *v* Australia, **1902**.

AY, eight for 13; and if tha'd been awake, it'd have been eight for 12.

EMMOTT ROBINSON replying to Alan Shackleton's congratulations after the latter had missed a half-chance at cover point, Yorkshire *v* Cambridge University.

IF I ever bowl a maiden over, it's not my fault.

ARTHUR MAILEY, Australian spin bowler.

THE dot ball has become the Holy Grail.

COLIN COWDREY, **1982**.

A straight ball has a certain lethal quality about it. If you miss it, you've 'ad it.

JIM SIMS, quoted in Mike Brearley, *The Art of Captaincy*, **1985**.

OCCUPATION: net bowler.

JACK BIRKENSHAW, Leicestershire all-rounder, filling in immigration cards during England's tour of India, **1972/3**.

THERE'S no rule against bowling fast.

CLIVE LLOYD, West Indies captain, **1985**.

WOULDN'T it be better if I got into the fridge?

QASIM OMAR, Pakistan batsman, receiving ice-pack treatment for bruising from Australian fast bowlers, Perth Test, **1983**.

I kept smiling at Thomson, hoping to keep him in a good mood.

RANJIT FERNANDO, 5 ft 2 in Sri Lankan batsman, as two of his team-mates were hospitalised by Jeff Thomson in a World Cup match, **1975**.

WATCHING the ski jumpers in flight is enough to convince me that perhaps the West Indies' fast bowling is fun after all.

DAVID GOWER at the Winter Olympics, **1988**.

Too high? If the ball had hit his head it would have hit his bloody wickets!

ALAN BROWN, Kent seam bowler, denied an lbw appeal against Lancashire batsman Harry Pilling (5 ft 3 ins).

LUCKIEST duck I ever made.

DON BRADMAN, after Aborigine Eddie Gilbert produced fastest speed he had ever faced, **1931**.

THANK God it wasn't twins!

HAMPSHIRE BATSMAN, on learning Larwood's wife had given birth to a daughter.

I suppose I can gain some consolation from the fact that my name will be permanently in the record books.

MALCOLM NASH, struck for six sixes in an over by Garfield Sobers, Glamorgan *v* Nottinghamshire at Swansea, **1968**.

Go on Hedley, you have him in two minds. He doesn't know whether to hit you for four or six.

ARTHUR WOOD, Yorkshire's wicket-keeper, to Hedley Verity at Bramall Lane as South African batsman H. B. Cameron took 30 off one over, **1935**.

MENTALLY, my stock ball pitches leg and hits off.

PHIL EDMONDS, from Simon Barnes' *A Singular Man*, **1986**.

YOU woke up in the night time and your arm was still going round.

L. O.'B. FLEETWOOD-SMITH, left-arm wrist spinner, heavily punished during Len Hutton's 364 *v* Australia at The Oval, **1938**. Hutton batted for 13 hrs 20 mins. (Fleetwood-Smith made his remarks on BBC Radio in **1970**.)

WHAT is the good of an innings of 50 if that man drops a couple of catches and lets by 40 or 50 runs? He has not only wiped his own runs off the slate, but he has probably upset the bowlers into the bargain.

A. E. R. GILLIGAN.

YOU don't expect to be beaten by a tail-ender – not at midnight anyway.

ROGER KNIGHT, beaten Gloucestershire captain, after late-night defeat in Gillette Cup tie *v* Lancashire at Old Trafford, **1971**.

You were simply caught in two-man's land.

KEN BARRINGTON to Brian Rose, on England's tour of West Indies, **1980**.

It's not easy to bat with tears in your eyes.

DON BRADMAN, bowled second ball by Eric Hollies after ovation in his last Test at The Oval, England v Australia, **1948**.

If I find your spectacles, I'll send them on to your mother.

GEOFFREY BOYCOTT's quip to Paul Allott, England team-mate, when he was asked to field at long leg during a bomb alert, Old Trafford Test, **1981**.

They'll shoot you in the leg so that they can get you lbw again.

KEITH FLETCHER to slip colleague Tony Lewis, in Bombay after PLO murder threat, MCC tour of India, **1972/3**.

'Ere, Rupert, you've got to hit the ball to be lbw in this game. If you miss it, you can only be caught.

KEITH FLETCHER, Essex captain, to Somerset's Peter Roebuck, **1981**.

Out if I hadn't hit it, well bowled, out if I hadn't hit it.

W. G. GRACE after he had kicked away a ball which was about to bowl him and added insult to injury by running a single.

And I suppose if anyone's bowled it's just a nasty accident?

GEORGE GUNN, on being told umpires would be generous with lbws during a festival match, **1920s**.

Shall we put our heads down and make runs, or get out quickly and make history?

DON SHEPHERD joining Peter Walker with Glamorgan 11–8 v Leicestershire, **1971**.

In England people do not speak to you unless they are firmly introduced with no hope of escape.

LEARIE CONSTANTINE in *Cricket in the Sun*.

THEY say the fool of the family always goes into the church.

TED DEXTER, referring to a series of run-out disasters involving Rev. David Sheppard, Australia *v* England, **1963**.

BAD luck, Peter lad. The Reverend has more chance than most of us when he puts his hands together.

REV. DAVID SHEPPARD's version of Fred Trueman's celebrated one-liner. This time in dressing room, after dismissal of Peter Parfitt, Gentlemen *v* Players, **1962**.

YOU'LL be no good with that stuff – you'll best get some ale down thee.

BRIAN JACKSON to Mike Hendrick in his early days in Derbyshire side.

No professional drunkard has ever made a great cricketer, nor ever will.

'QUID' in *Jerks from Short Leg*, **1866**.

WHAT, indeed, should I do at a dance with my dumpling of a person tumbling about like a cricket ball on uneven ground?

MARY RUSSELL MITFORD, first woman cricket writer.

I would rather go to a pub with half a dozen Northern professionals than to all the studios, penthouses or Athaeneums and Saville Clubs in London.

NEVILLE CARDUS.

THAT'S the end of cricket for me. I think I'll start running a discotheque.

MUDASSAR after being given out lbw, Pakistan *v* England, **1978**. (Quoted in Wasim Bari's diary.)

I was too old for discos when I was 12.

BOB WILLIS, **1983**.

I don't try to be Joe Blow, the super-stud – it just happens.

JEFF THOMSON, from *Thommo*, **1981**.

GIVEN the choice between Raquel Welch and a hundred at Lord's I'd take the hundred every time.

GEOFFREY BOYCOTT, **1981**.

I have played my best cricket when I have been with my wife. If wives are accepted into the happy family, things will be very much better.

ALAN KNOTT, **1977**.

CRICKET is like sex films – they relieve frustration and tension.

LINDA LOVELACE, star of *Deep Throat*, visiting Lord's for England *v* India Test, **1974**.

ENGLAND'S always expecting. No wonder they call her the Mother Country.

FRED TRUEMAN on being asked for a final effort in a Test match.

THE season of 1896 was to me one of vast interest. It marked my first acquaintance with Plato and Fenner's.

G. L. JESSOP.

IT was Jung, I think, who said we learned from our failures, success merely confirming us in our mistakes. What can I learn from my failures at Test level?

MIKE BREARLEY, **1981**.

I make no pretensions to oratory and I'd any day as soon make a duck as a speech.

W. G. GRACE, *Cricketing Reminiscences*, **1899**.

Mr Mayor and Gentlemen, I can't make a speech beyond saying thank you but I'm ready to box any man in the room three rounds.

J. W. H. T. DOUGLAS, England cricketer and Olympic gold medallist at boxing, tour of Australia, **1911/12**.

I'D rather face Dennis Lillee with a stick of rhubarb than go through all that again.

IAN BOTHAM, cleared of assault at Grimsby Crown Court, **1981**.

IT always seemed to me that cricket would be a better game if the papers didn't publish the averages.

JACK HOBBS, from John Arlott's *Jack Hobbs: Profile of The Master*, **1981**.

THE only things that really keep me going are statistics.

RICHARD HADLEE, *At the Double*, **1985**.

My word, Herbert, if it hadn't been for my lumbago, we'd have brayed 'em.

PERCY HOLMES (224) to Herbert Sutcliffe (313) after world-record partnership of 555 for first wicket *v* Essex at Leyton, **1932**.

THE scoreboard is an ass.

SIR NEVILLE CARDUS, *A Fourth Innings with Cardus*, **1981**.

THE essence, the aristocracy of 0 is that it should be surrounded by large scores, that it should resemble the little silent bread-winner in a bus full of fat, noisy women. Indeed, when the years have fixed it in its place, so far from being merely the foil to jewels, it should itself grow, in the fond eye of memory, to the shape and stature of a gem.

R. C. ROBERTSON-GLASGOW, on the delight of making nought.

PEOPLE say, do you think you would have played for England if you'd started at 18? And I say, I might. And I might have been sacked by Lancashire when I was 19 and all.

JACK SIMMONS, **1985**.

PEOPLE don't pay to watch me any more. They come to see me drop dead from exhaustion or old age.

BILL ALLEY, Somerset all-rounder, **1967**.

I'M going while you still ask why. I'm not waiting until you ask why not.

PATSY HENDREN, Middlesex and England batsman, on reason for his retirement.

THERE comes a time when a man must realise that his cricket days are over. The thing first began to dawn on me when I noticed that the captain of the side, whenever he started to set his fielders, invariably began by saying, 'General, will you go point?'

BRIDAGIER-GENERAL HUGH HEADLAM in *The Times*, **1930**.

THEY say spinners mature with age. I am just hoping they are right.

JOHN CHILDS on his England call-up at 36, **1988**.

WHEN he asked me if I could turn out, I thought he wanted me to play him at golf.

FRED TITMUS, after a phone call from Don Bennett, Middlesex secretary, with a recall at the age of 46, **1979**.

GOLF is a game to be played between cricket and death.

COLIN INGLEBY-MACKENZIE, ex-Hampshire captain.

I got bowled by a slow full toss, and I knew something was wrong with my eyes.

WILFRED RHODES, playing in Scotland a year after his retirement, **1931**.

AH well, my feet aren't what they used to be.

HAROLD LARWOOD, awarded nought for plenty in a computer test 'played' at Lord's between England and Australia, **1971**.

I'M off to another world, via the bat room.

AUBREY FAULKNER, of South Africa, in a suicide note he left before gassing himself, **1930**.

I see that Northamptonshire have a new bowler called Kettle. May I suggest to Keith Andrew that the best time to put him on would be ten minutes before the tea interval?

LETTER in *The Cricketer*, **1959**.

I want to play cricket; it does not seem to matter whether you win or lose.

MEATLOAF, US rock singer, **1984**.

PAVILION steps are the last place you expect to meet a car. You get a few knocks playing cricket, but never anything like this.

PAUL KINGSBURY, Endon batsman, after being knocked over by a car driven by an opponent, **1986**. Kingsbury lost 3 pints of blood.

DERYCK Murray has batted well; he is the nigger in the woodpile as far as the English are concerned.

BRIAN JOHNSTON, **1980.**

THE question of South Africa has been the nigger in the woodpile.

KEN TURNER, Northamptonshire secretary, talking about the English cricketers' tour of South Africa, **1982**.

THAT's cricket, old sport.

FRANK BRUNO, following knockout victory against South African Gerrie Coetzee in a world heavyweight title eliminator in London, **1986**.

7

Close Encounters

South Africa and Apartheid

FELLOW sportsmen say to me, 'I'm a sportsman, apartheid is nothing to do with me.' Does that mean they are sportsmen even before human beings? Well, I'm a sportsman second and a human being first.

JOHN ABRAHAMS, Lancashire's Cape Coloured batsman, **1988**.

A few days ago John Carlisle and Norris McWhirter were in court, arguing about principles. They spoke in high-falutin' terms about freedom. It's a pity that they don't set equality of races as high as the freedom of 300 county cricketers.

PETER ROEBUCK, *Sunday Times*, **1989**.

WE just hope that Governments are now prepared to play ball. After all, I would like to think that they will respect a unanimous decision.

LORD BRAMALL, MCC president and chairman of ICC, after world's cricketing nations voted in **1989** to impose bans on players going to South Africa.

IT is the Governments of the cricket-playing countries who will determine whether cricket is played in these territories, not the Cricket Boards.

ARMON ADAMS, Guyana's first Secretary in London.

THEY can get £20,000 for having their heads knocked off in the West Indies or £60,000 for two tours of South Africa.

JACK BANNISTER, secretary of the Players Association, on the choice likely to be facing English cricketers after ICC sanctions against South Africa, **1989**.

JACK Bannister's contribution is disturbing. He is predicting, if not advocating, rebel tours. He also works for South African television, so his independence is open to question. It is not fit that the secretary of the players' association is so closely tied to South African interests.

PETER ROEBUCK, **1989**.

THE citizens of the United Kingdom have had a freedom curtailed at the insistence of other countries.

GRAEME WRIGHT, editor, *Wisden*, **1989**, on the ICC agreement not to pick players who had been to South Africa.

THE price of blackmail is eternal ransom and they may live to regret it in future. Foreign Governments must be taught that whatever restrictions they place on their own citizens, we still live in a free country.

NORRIS MCWHIRTER, chairman of Freedom Association, opposing ICC's South African restrictions, **1989**.

THIS will mean even more money knocking around to play in South Africa.

MIKE GATTING, in **1989**. He later took some of it himself.

ALREADY speculation is rife about how many England players are prepared to sell themselves to the Republic. Who knows what damage it could do to the strength of the England team due to tour the Caribbean next winter?

DAVID GOWER, **1989**.

FEW of those within the world of first-class cricket are political animals. That, however, is no excuse for being politically unconscious.

JOHN ARLOTT on D'Oliveira affair, **1968**.

SORRY, I can't say anything at the moment. My comment is in the car.

ANONYMOUS REBEL TOURIST replying to press query about his reasons for going to South Africa, **1989**.

I was disgusted by the crowd's reaction. I am here to play cricket.
Politics are nothing to do with me.

ALVIN KALLICHARRAN, West Indies batsman, after hostile reception from black
section of Capetown crowd, **1982**.

THERE can be no normal sport in an abnormal society.

Stance of South African Cricket Board, who run non-white competitions.

ALL I know is there is a nice golf course there.

ALEC BEDSER, chairman of selectors, when asked about intricacies of Gleneagles
Agreement at height of Robin Jackman affair; tour of West Indies, **1980/81**.

SOUTH Africa should never have had Test status. The South African
Cricket Association does not represent the whole country. It is a
fact that the Association practised rigid apartheid long before the
government required it and they show no desire to end it.

DENNIS BRUTUS, Secretary of the non-white South African Sports Association,
1960.

IF the game can conceivably be used as a force to unite conflicting
racial groups, there seems to be no reason by South African cricket
should not recover from its present malaise.

J. P. FELLOWS-SMITH after the disastrous **1960** tour of England was followed by
South Africa's withdrawal from the Commonwealth and consequent loss of ICC
membership.

ALL our sportsmen have proved they are willing to meet players
from any land provided it does not conflict with the policies over
which they have no say.

JACK CHEETHAM, former South Africa captain, on the ICC decision to defer the
question of his country's readmittance to the ICC after leaving the Commonwealth.

SOME of those who said I should have kept my mouth shut held that a parson should only speak about religion . . . such men want to think of life as a series of watertight compartments. 'Don't let your home life affect your business life. Don't let your business life affect your sport. Don't let religion affect the way you run the other parts of your life.' But the whole point is that, if Christ is Lord, there are no other parts of life.

REV. DAVID SHEPPARD, on speaking out against cricketing links with South Africa in *Parson's Pitch*, **1964**.

WE will never know the whole truth concerning the omission of D'Oliveira from the MCC touring party to South Africa. . . . I come down on the side of honesty, a good honest piece of bungling by good honest men.

TED DEXTER's verdict as Cape coloured Basil D'Oliveira was first omitted, and then chosen, for MCC's tour of South Africa, **1968**.

THINKING of you very much today. Love to you both, Penny Cowdrey.

Inscription on bouquet of flowers after D'Oliveira was not chosen; her husband, Colin, was captain.

GUESTS who have ulterior motives usually find they are not invited.

VORSTER, South African Prime Minister, when hearing that Basil D'Oliveira, overlooked in England's tour party, intended to cover series as a journalist, **1968**.

IT's not the MCC team. It's the team of the anti-apartheid movement. We are not prepared to have a team thrust upon us.

VORSTER, when D'Oliveira was drafted into MCC tour party in place of injured Tom Cartwright, **1968**.

THE selectors' brief throughout was simply to choose the best available team on cricket merit.

MCC statement on D'Oliveira affair, **1968**.

I wanted to be a cricketer who had been chosen as a cricketer and not as a symbol.

BASIL D'OLIVEIRA in *The D'Oliveira Affair*, **1968**.

WHAT has been done is tantamount to punching a wife for the crimes of her husband.

PETER POLLOCK, South African pace bowler, on the cancellation of their England tour, **1970**.

YOU do not cut yourself off from friends.

RAMAN SUBBA ROW, pressing for South Africa tour of England to go ahead, **1970**.

I'M ashamed I was so late in coming to the realisation of the South African evil.

REV. DAVID SHEPPARD, Bishop of Woolwich, **1970**.

THE triumph of the campus bums.

THE CONSERVATIVE PARTY's Monday Club on the cancellation of South Africa's tour of England, **1970**, after student demonstrations.

WHY should we allow our boys to be insulted by those long-haired louts?

B. J. SCHOEMAN, South African Minister for Transport, supporting cancellation of South African tour to England, **1970**.

I would always speak to a demonstrator, provided he was polite.

ALI BACHER, South African captain, prior to cancellation of tour to England, **1970**.

THE Council see no reason to repeat the arguments, to which they still adhere, which led them to sustain the invitation to the South African cricketers issued four years ago. They do, however, deplore the activities of those who by the intimidation of individual cricketers and threats of violent disruption have inflamed the whole issue.

LAST PARAGRAPH of Cricket Council statement, 22 May, reluctantly announcing cancellation of SA tour after pressure from Labour Government, **1970**.

WE cricketers feel that the time has come for an expression of our views. We fully support the South African Cricket Association's application to include non-whites on the tour to Australia if good enough and, furthermore, subscribe to merit being the only criterion on the cricket field.

STATEMENT by South African players at Newlands, in Transvaal v Rest of South Africa match, after walk-off in protest against the government's refusal to allow integrated cricket, **1971**.

THAT list is of no importance.

ROBIN JACKMAN on the United Nations' blacklist of players who had visited South Africa, **1981**.

EVERY phone that I am talking to you on is listened to.

IAN BOTHAM, England captain, during deportation of Robin Jackman from Guyana for South African links. England's tour of West Indies, **1981**.

IT's a great honour, but it will not make any difference about my decision not to be available to tour India this winter.

GRAHAM GOOCH, on becoming England's fourth captain of the series v West Indies, **1988**.

IT seems obvious they don't want to play in India.

MARGARET ALVA, India's Minister for Sport, after Gooch withdrew from his South African commitment to lead the England touring team. The **1988/9** tour was cancelled.

WOULDN'T you go to Russia or China if it was a free trip with all expenses paid?

GEOFFREY BOYCOTT during England's tour of India, explaining that he would still visit South Africa, **1981**.

WHEN I toured South Africa with Oxbridge Jazzhats, I became physically ill for a week. We were being used for propaganda. I will never return there.

DEREK PRINGLE, **1982**.

I'VE got nothing on my conscience. I'm just here to play cricket.

PETER WILLEY on English rebel tour to South Africa, **1982**.

THEY are being used as political pawns and have succumbed to greed.

KEN TURNER, Northants secretary, **1982**.

BEING a Christian I cannot imagine a missionary saying: 'We won't go there until apartheid is finished.'

ALAN KNOTT, explaining why he joined South African rebel tour, in *It's Knott Cricket*, **1985**.

ISN'T he the one who is a traitor?

SMALL BOY about Graham Gooch at Essex benefit match, in the wake of South African rebel tour, **1982**.

How can you play cricket with a bloke and then not be allowed to sit in a railway carriage with him?

KEN MCEWAN, on the ordering out of West Indian Colin Croft from a 'whites-only' section of South African train, **1983**.

ROD felt there were more things to life than playing cricket for his country.

DONNA MCCURDY, wife of Rod McCurdy, Australian pace bowler who joined rebel South African tour, **1985**.

THAT man's got to appreciate it's a sensitive situation. He's a white man who has played in South Africa and he can't shout at a black man in the West Indies.

LOCKHART SEBASTIEN, of Windward Islands, after Greg Thomas challenged a batsman to 'walk'. England tour, **1986**.

GOBBLEDEGOOCH.

SOUTH AFRICAN NEWSPAPER headline on Gooch's statement which overcame West Indian objections to his inclusion in the England tour party, **1986**.

APARTHEID kept us back and restricted our opportunities. I watched white cricketers and stole from them with my eyes.

OMAR HENRY, first coloured cricketer to represent South Africa, **1987**.

IF I'd known what was in store, I'd never have played the sport.

OMAR HENRY discussing his rift with other coloured players, **1986**.

I understood that people could demonstrate peacefully and obviously I would be unhappy if it was peaceful and it was still dispersed in such a way.

MIKE GATTING, after a demonstration at Jan Smuts airport, Johannesburg, protesting against the arrival of the British rebels had been dispersed with dogs and teargas, **1990**.

Bodyline

I don't want to see you Mr Warner. There are two teams out there; one is trying to play cricket and the other is not.

BILL WOODFULL, Australian captain to Pelham Warner, the England manager, during Adelaide Test, **1932/3** series.

BODYLINE bowling has assumed such proportions as to menace the best interests of the game, making protection of the body by the batsmen the main consideration. This is causing intensely bitter feeling between the players as well as injury. In our opinion it is unsportsmanlike. Unless stopped at once it is likely to upset the friendly relationships existing between Australia and England

TEXT OF CABLE from Australian Cricket Board to MCC, following Adelaide Test, **1933**.

WE, Marylebone Cricket Club, deplore your cable. We deprecate your opinion that there has been unsportsmanlike play. We have fullest confidence in captain, team and managers and are convinced they would do nothing to infringe either the Laws of Cricket or the game. We have no evidence that our confidence has been misplaced. Much as we regret the accidents to Woodfull and Oldfield, we understand that in neither case was the bowler to blame. If the Australian Board of Control wish to propose a new Law or Rule, it shall receive our careful consideration in due course.

We hope the situation is now not as serious as your cable would seem to indicate, but if it is such as to jeopardise the good relations between England and Australian cricketers and you consider it desirable to cancel remainder of programme, we would consent, but with great reluctance.

MCC's cabled reply, **1933**.

> We have fought
> We have won
> And we have lost
> But we have never squealed before.

EARL OF DARTMOUTH, MCC elder statesman, putting his feelings into verse after arrival of Australian telegram. (Quoted in *Cricket and Empire*, Sissons and Stoddart, **1984**.)

LEG theory is generally a confession of impotence on the part of a bowler, and that should serve to cut it out of the game of any and every bowler claiming to be first class.

THE CRICKETER, **1925**.

IF that little bugger can do that to him, what might I do?

HAROLD LARWOOD, watching Gubby Allen dismiss Don Bradman cheaply, England *v* Australia, **1930**.

WELL, we shall win the Ashes – but we may lose a Dominion.

ROCKLEY WILSON, Winchester cricket coach, upon hearing that Jardine would captain MCC in Australia, **1932/3**.

BOWES should alter his tactics. He bowled with five men on the on-side, and sent down several very short-pitched balls which repeatedly bounced head high and more. This is not bowling, indeed it is not cricket, and if all the fast bowlers were to adopt his methods there would be trouble and plenty of it.

EDITORIAL in *The Cricketer*, shortly before Bowes was drafted into England squad for the Bodyline series, **1932/3**.

IF we don't beat you, we'll knock your bloody heads off.

BILL VOCE, England paceman, to Australia's Vic Richardson at the start of the Bodyline series, **1932/3**.

WELL bowled, Harold!

D. R. JARDINE to Larwood as he hit Woodfull above the heart in Adelaide Test.

HIS Excellency is a conscientious objector.

DOUGLAS JARDINE'S remark when Nawab of Pataudi refused to join the leg-side field, Bodyline series, **1932/3**.

IF I happen to get hit out there Dad, keep Mum from jumping the fence and laying into those Pommy bowlers.

STAN MCCABE, resuming his innings of 187 in the Bodyline series, **1932/3**.

WHAT about those fellows who marched to Kandahar with the fever on them?

DOUGLAS JARDINE's reply to Plum Warner, when informed that Eddie Paynter, Lancashire batsman, was in hospital and could miss the Test.

No politics ever introduced in the British Empire ever caused me so much trouble as this damn Bodyline bowling.

J. H. THOMAS, Secretary of State for the Dominions, during a luncheon speech at Claridges, **1933**.

I would rather lose the rubber than win over the bruised bodies of my opponents.

RANJITSINHJI, condemning Bodyline tactics, **1933**.

BATSMEN, particularly those who opened the innings for both countries since the First World War, had brought the trouble on themselves. In every dressing-room we heard the warning given by captains to opening batsmen: 'If you nibble at anything outside the off-stump, you'll get a good kick in the pants when you come back – even if you score a century.'

ARTHUR MAILEY on the background to Bodyline.

LEG THEORY, even as bowled by Larwood, came as a natural evolution in the game. There was nothing sinister about it and nothing sinister was intended.

BILL BOWES, *Express Deliveries*. **1949**.

I'M sure my father wasn't a pisspot and a yobbo as portrayed.

JANE LARWOOD on the TV series *Bodyline*, **1985**.

Throwing

THE straight-armed bowling, introduced by John Willes, Esq., was generally practised in this game, and proved a great obstacle against getting runs in comparison to what might have been got by straightforward bowling.

MORNING POST report on 23 of Kent *v* 13 of England, **1807**. (Quoted in H. S. Altham and E. W. Swanton, *A History of Cricket*, 1962.)

WILLES threw down the ball in disgust, jumped on his horse, and rode away out of Lord's and out of cricket history.

ALTHAM AND SWANTON on Willes being no-balled by Noah Mann, MCC *v* Kent, **1822**, in *A History of Cricket*, 1962.

THE elegant and scientific game of cricket will degenerate into a mere exhibition of rough, coarse, horse-play.

JOHN NYREN on the consequences of allowing round-arm bowling.

FAR more latitude seems to be allowed to bowlers in England than in the Colonies, where unfair bowling is at once put down.

JOHN CONWAY, manager of the Australian touring team, **1878**, complaining about the prevalence of 'chuckers' in Yorkshire.

I was twice bowled by Nash in Ephraim Lockwood's benefit match. Nash was just a real Lancashire 'chucker', slow left; but even if he had been fast no-one in those days seemed capable of even attempting to stop throwing. It was not until later that Lord Harris took a most worthy stand against this abuse, and thank goodness he did, or throwing might have been carried on to the present day.

LORD HAWKE, on his first 'pair' in **1882**, in *Recollections and Reminiscences*, 1924.

FAST bowlers get massage in the back; Eddie got it in the crook of the arm.

SYD REDGRAVE of Queensland, on questionable action of his colleague Eddie Gilbert, Aborigine fast bowler, after his bouncers had hit three batsmen, **1935**.

WAS I bowled or run out?

> DOUG INSOLE, bowled by Tony Lock's quicker ball, The Rest *v* Surrey, The Oval, **1955**.

IF they stop throwing, cricket in Australia will die.

> TOMMY ANDREWS, former Australian Test player, **1958/9** Test series.

BOWL him one for a change Burkie, you'll surprise him.

> COLLEAGUE to Burke, New South Wales bowler, during throwing controversy in Australia; MCC tour, **1957/8**.

To bowl fast is a gift given to very few; traditionally only to those with either a vast body or a long flexible arm. Now we see thin men, unco-ordinated men, ordinary men, qualifying as fast bowlers.

> ROBIN MARLAR on the effects of throwing, *The Cricketer*, **1960**.

YES, I'm the last of the straight-arm bowlers.

> RAY LINDWALL replying to Bill Bowes' congratulations on his selection for Australia *v* England, **1958/9**.

ONE can readily appreciate Buller's predicament, and one cannot question his right to act as he did, but it was ironic that his action should be taken at a time when the players were engaged in a light-hearted knock about.

> *THE CRICKETER* editorial, July **1960**, on the no-balling of Geoff Griffin (S. Africa) for throwing in the knock-up game at Lord's after the Test's early finish.

No umpire enjoys calling bowlers for throwing. It is a very unpleasant task . . . but someone has to stop illegal bowling.

> TOM SMITH, General Secretary of the Association of Cricket Umpires, in *The Cricketer*, July **1960**.

THROWING is unfair. It is insidious, infectious and a menace to the game. It must be stopped and the exchange of cables between countries will not do it. Unless it is stopped before the Australians arrive, a serious position is imminent.

TOM SMITH, *The Cricketer*, July **1960**.

YOU must be the greatest thrower-out of all time, but I think your action is suspect.

KEN 'SLASHER' MACKAY to Joe Soloman for the run-out which tied the Australian *v* West Indies Test match, **1960/61**.

IF his action is the same as it was, he would be no-balled walking down the gangplank at Tilbury.

ENGLAND PLAYER on Meckiff's illegal action, **1963**.

HIS [Meckiff's] selection represents one of the most fantastic somersaults in cricket policies in our time.

W. J. O'REILLY on the recall of Meckiff for the Australia *v* South Africa Tests of **1963/4** after the throwing controversy.

I think our selectors have insulted South Africa by this move. All Meckiff's team-mates, though once divided, now agree he infringes Law 26.

RAY LINDWALL.

I do not support the selection of men who do not play to the rules.

CLEM JONES, Lord Mayor of Brisbane and Queensland representative on the Australian Board of Control.

I bowled Meckiff for hundreds of overs before umpires who approved his delivery and I have accepted their decision. Now that an umpire does not accept Meckiff's delivery, I accept that decision too, I will not bowl him again.

RICHIE BENAUD, Australian captain, after Meckiff had been no-balled for throwing in the First Test, Australia *v* South Africa at Brisbane, **1963/4**.

I know that Richie did the right thing, because he is behind every player.

IAN MECKIFF on Benaud's decision to take him off after he was no-balled in his first over.

IT defies description – the feeling that hits players when there is a no-ball called for throwing. . . . One can only assume that the game was carried on by instinct for a while, for the Australian players were not . . . 'with it'.

RICHIE BENAUD after Meckiff had been called at Brisbane.

I'M afraid this is the end, Dad.

RICHIE BENAUD to Ian Meckiff after the latter had been no-balled for throwing, Australia v South Africa, **1961/2**.

IF they re-write the Laws and say that double-jointed people must not be allowed to play the first-class game, well, fair enough.

HAROLD RHODES, Derbyshire paceman, during throwing controversy, **1966**.

The Packer Circus

CRICKET is the easiest sport in the world to take over. Nobody bothered to pay the players what they were worth.

KERRY PACKER, **1977**.

THE whole basis of this is an ideal – but nobody is going to do it for peanuts.

TONY GREIG, England captain, revealing plans for Packer series at a press conference, Hove, **1977**.

THE plight of the modern cricketer is certainly not the best. Many who've been playing eight years or more are living on the breadline. In the winter they go abroad coaching, leaving their families behind. Test cricketers are also not paid what they're worth. As a result of this action, cricket may in five or ten years come into line with tennis and golf. Then, if a young man is faced with a decision which to play, he can choose cricket with confidence. People who give up their lives to a game should be rewarded accordingly.

TONY GREIG, at same Hove press conference, 1977.

IT makes me laugh when I hear the anti-Packer lobby telling me how to spend my winters. When I was a teenager, the same sort of people did not give a damn what I did between September and April.

GORDON GREENIDGE, 1980.

THE administrators have had 100 years to improve pay and conditions for the players and they haven't made any progress.

MUSHTAQ MOHAMMED in Peter McFarline's A Game Divided, 1977.

I have no desire to be a hack bowler up the bush with Packer.

RODNEY HOGG, Australian quickie, 1978.

IT was always 'Kerry says this' and 'Kerry says that', like a speak-your-weight machine.

BOB TAYLOR on Packer players in Standing Up, Standing Back, 1985.

IN affectionate remembrance of International Cricket, which died at Hove, 9th May, 1977. Deeply lamented by a large circle of friends and acquaintances. R.I.P. NB – The body will be cremated and the Ashes taken to Australia and scattered around the studio of TCN9 in Sydney – NTJCBM.

NOTICE placed by three Australian journalists in The Times, 1977.

HIS action has inevitably impaired the trust which existed between the cricket authorities and the captain of the England side.

TCCB cricket council, upon sacking Tony Greig as England's captain after announcement of Packer Circus, **1977**.

WHEN I went into this I knew I was putting my captaincy on the line and I think that was very unselfish of me.

TONY GREIG, accused of selling out by joining Packer, **1977**.

THERE is a little bit of the whore in all of us, gentlemen, don't you think?

KERRY PACKER, meeting Australian Board of Control to discuss TV rights, **1976**.

FROM now on, it is every man for himself and let the devil take the hindmost.

KERRY PACKER, leaving ICC meeting at Lord's, **1977**.

I'VE read a lot about Genghis Khan. He wasn't very lovable. But he was bloody efficient.

KERRY PACKER, **1977**.

IT's unfortunate we Australians inherited the English mentality rather than the American.

KERRY PACKER, the *Guardian*, **1977**.

YOU British reckon everything can be solved by compromise and diplomacy. We Australians fight to the very last ditch.

KERRY PACKER, **1978**.

THEY are dedicated lovers of the game who nevertheless found it hard fully to understand the feelings and aspirations of those who seek to make their livings out of it.

MR JUSTICE SLADE, about the cricketing establishment, during High Court ruling that ban on Packer players was illegal, **1977**.

I'VE heard the only way to get out of a Packer contract is to become
pregnant.

> RAY STEELE, treasurer of Australian Cricket Board, during High Court hearing on
> Packer Affair, **1977**.

TESTS are not built in a day.

> MUTTHIAN CHIDAMBARAN (India), High Court.

THEY want the penny and the bun.

> GEOFFREY BOYCOTT, High Court.

WARS are not won by appeasement.

> W. H. WEBSTER, chairman of ICC, High Court.

WAKE up, you lazy lot! You've got to get used to this daytime
cricket!

> MUSHTAQ MOHAMMED to World XI colleagues on bus taking them to a rare morning
> start in Packer's World Series, **1978**.

I do not know that Test cricket can be saved. I hope so but I am not
convinced. People will no longer sit through five days of a match.
Those days are long gone. People don't go to watch beautiful
defensive shots or the battle of tactics any more. Unless something
is done to change the rules and the manner in which it is played, then
officials will have a hard time to make it attractive.

> LYNTON TAYLOR, Channel 9 executive, **1978**.

SIR – An electrician recently came into my office to mend the fire
alarm. Finding a broken wire he said 'Look at this, it's kerried.' I
asked what he meant and he replied 'It's Kerry Packered –
knackered!'

> LETTER in *Wisden Cricket Monthly*, **1980**.

Civil Wars

1 Yorkshire

WE are a magnificent and united club and no one is going to say any different.

REG KIRK, Yorkshire chairman, on the day Brian Close resigned as cricket chairman, **1984**.

FOR years I have said that Yorkshire is run by a lot of people who think their old-fashioned methods are good enough to cope with modern cricket. A rot has set in with Yorkshire. And it's eating away the greatest county club in the world.

JOHNNY WARDLE, sacked by Yorkshire, **1958**.

A dark thundercloud seems to have descended upon this club, clouding the thoughts of those running the club in the day-to-day affairs and affecting the players' team spirit. There are those who have been grabbed by an overriding passion to proliferate their own desires. The situation cannot be allowed to continue. It is destroying what used to be a great cricket club.

VISCOUNT MOUNTGARRET, maiden speech as Yorkshire president at annual meeting in Leeds, **1985**.

THE Yorkshire County Cricket Club has behaved like the Labour Party in its worst periods. Every time there's a little dispute, everybody attacks each other in public.

ROY HATTERSLEY, Labour Party politician, **1983**.

IT is not likely to be possible to pass fair judgement on the cricketers of Yorkshire, *qua* cricketers, until the club has undergone radical heart surgery.

JOHN ARLOTT, **1984**.

YORKSHIRE sacked me because I refused to accept the authority of the quite hopeless old man appointed captain.

JOHNNY WARDLE, after sacking by Yorkshire, **1958**. Ronnie Burnet was the captain.

MAYBE I swore with justification. Often they were the sort of catches that could have been taken comfortably had the offender been in bed at the same time as I was.

JOHNNY WARDLE, accused by Clifford Hesketh, chairman of Yorkshire's selection committee, of bad language towards team-mates, **1958**.

HE may be good enough for England, but not for Yorkshire.

BRIAN SELLERS, defending Yorkshire's decision to sack Johnny Wardle four days after his selection to join the MCC tour of Australia, **1957**.

LET him go then, and he can take any other bugger who feels t'same way.

BRIAN SELLERS after Ray Illingworth's 'contract or I'll leave' ultimatum to Yorkshire, **1968**.

WELL Brian, you've had a good innings. I'm going to give you the option of resigning or getting the sack.

BRIAN SELLERS, Yorkshire's cricket chairman, to Brian Close, **1970**.

HIS removal will have to be handled as delicately as a military operation.

YORKSHIRE COMMITTEE MAN, planning removal of Geoffrey Boycott from county captaincy, **1971**.

I could not time the ball. I did what others have done often enough in the past.

JOHN HAMPSHIRE, after his infamous go-slow v. Northampton, **1978**.

THEY are small-minded people – people who think they are always right. The whole thing was a set-up. They knew they were going to sack me, but at least they could have postponed the meeting. They could have allowed my mother to be buried in peace but they could not wait.

GEOFFREY BOYCOTT to Michael Parkinson, BBC Television, after sacking as Yorkshire's captain, **1978**.

IF they want me to return as captain, they must do something about it. They have got to get together, get off their bottoms and do what they have to do to make it happen.

GEOFFREY BOYCOTT.

IT is not for what you have done but because of what you are.

ARTHUR CONNELL, Yorkshire's chairman, informing Geoffrey Boycott why he had lost the county captaincy, **1978**.

IT's about time they buried the hatchet – and in the garden, not in one another's backs.

MICHAEL CRAWFORD, Yorkshire chairman, announcing Boycott, Illingworth and Old would remain with club, **1982**.

THE situation is a smaller version of the United States and Russia. They have their differences but they still have to live on the same planet. We have to realise that we have to live on the planet, too.

MICHAEL CRAWFORD on the county's interminable cricket war.

MY lasting memory will be of the greatest of all counties reduced to a squabbling rabble, of squalid, petty argument, of supporters, once the most loyal and sane of all memberships, torn apart by a cult which regarded one man as greater than the club.

JOHN HAMPSHIRE on his feelings as he left Yorkshire for Derbyshire, in *Family Argument*, **1983**.

I don't know of another club in history which finished bottom of the league, sacked its star player and left the manager in the job. The Yorkshire committee are guilty of the biggest whitewash I can ever recall.

BRIAN CLOUGH on the sacking of Geoffrey Boycott, **1983**.

WHEN anyone tells me that so-and-so is indispensable, I always reply, 'I know, the churchyard's full of 'em.'

FRED TRUEMAN, defending sacking of Geoffrey Boycott, **1983**.

I am happy and relieved at the outcome, I accept the members' offer to me with joy and humility and will do my best to be worthy of the confidence and affection shown towards me.

GEOFFREY BOYCOTT, reinstated as a Yorkshire player following members' vote of 'no confidence' in county committee, **1984**.

THIS decision is a triumph for non-cricketers over cricketers.

SIR LEN HUTTON after overthrow of Yorkshire committee which attempted to sack Geoffrey Boycott, **1984**.

RAY will find it rather strange joining us after all he has been through in recent years. He's joining a team where all the players actually talk to and like each other.

FRED TRUEMAN welcoming sacked Yorkshire manager Ray Illingworth to the Old England charity-match cricket team, **1984**.

GEOFF has only two points of view. You are either for him or against him. There is no middle ground.

BRIAN CLOSE, resigning as Yorkshire's cricket chairman because he claimed committee was dominated by Geoffrey Boycott, **1984**.

I would like him to resign but I don't think there's an earthly chance of him doing so.

SID FIELDEN, on Geoffrey Boycott's dual role as player and committee man, **1984**.

WE are a cricket club, not a debating society.

> DAVID BAIRSTOW, Yorkshire captain, **1985**.

WE might not have done much good for Yorkshire cricket but we could have helped a few people with their personal problems.

> YORKSHIRE TV PRODUCER, reacting to the embarrassing British Telecom mix-up which followed a debate over the future of Yorkshire cricket. Viewers trying to phone in with comments were treated to a recorded message on how to maintain an erection, **1989**.

IF the club had handled it right they could have filled the ground. But they hadn't done things properly for 124 years so there was no reason why they should start.

> GEOFFREY BOYCOTT in **1989**, recalling his last day as a Yorkshire player at Scarborough three years earlier.

IT was a huff and puff meeting. Nothing ever gets done. They want to make me the whipping boy, and it won't work.

> GEOFFREY BOYCOTT, after flouncing out of a Yorkshire committee meeting, called in response to the county's second-from-bottom finish in **1989**. Boycott had been accused of having nothing constructive to offer.

2   Somerset

As far as I'm concerned, you are part of the buildings and the furniture at Somerset and so are Vic and Ian. . . . I hope that you'll be able to play with us until those legs turn to jelly, because I think that you and I and Ian and Vic are Somerset players right down to our bootstraps.

> PETER ROEBUCK's letter to Viv Richards on his appointment as Somerset captain for the **1986** season.

WHEN you have two work horses and shoot them in the back, I think it's evil. You don't treat animals in this way. I was blindfolded, led up an alley and assassinated.

> VIV RICHARDS on hearing in August **1986** that Somerset were not renewing his contract.

SACKING Viv Richards is like sending Shergar to Argentina for dog meat.

IAN BOTHAM, **1986**.

I could see they were lost; they had no sense of direction, no sense of purpose, no pride, they were drifting. The club had no leadership.

MARTIN CROWE on state of Somerset's young players prior to sacking of Richards and Garner, **1986**.

IT is always hard to cut down a huge tree, let alone three.

MARTIN CROWE in **1986**. The three trees were Viv Richards, Joel Garner and Ian Botham. Somerset cut down the first two; the third subsequently uprooted himself.

I don't take back a word of what I said. But over the season my feelings changed.

ROEBUCK in October **1986**.

THIS committee has done for fair play what Colonel Gadaffi has done for air safety.

JAN FOLEY, Bristol barrister, putting the Somerset rebels' case at the Somerset special general meeting, **1986**.

WE had great difficulty this summer in getting him [Richards] to play in our evening pub games – he declined to play at Clevedon, Truro and Braunton, and the only reason he played at Ottery St Mary was that we reminded him that they had staged a benefit match for him the year before.

MICHAEL HILL, Somerset chairman, defending the committee decision, **1986**.

I'M told that Peter Roebuck is flying out to have a man-to-man talk with me. I suggest he stays in London. He'll be a whole lot safer there.

IAN BOTHAM on hearing the confirmation of Somerset's decision to sack Richards and Garner while in Australia.

8

Lords and Masters

MCC, Selectors, Committees and Others

THEY bring him out of the loft, take the dust sheet off, give him a pink gin and sit him there. He can't go out of a 30-mile radius of London because he's normally too pissed to get back. He sits there at Lord's, saying 'That's Botham, look at his hair, they tell me he's had some of that cannabis stuff.'

IAN BOTHAM, speaking at a cricket dinner, describing a typical England selector, **1986**.

I'M not anti-Establishment per se. I'm anti-stupidity.

PETER ROEBUCK, **1989**.

DISRAELI once stated that a country lives by its institutions. This is certainly true of Great Britain; it is full of institutions. Some, like the Royal National Lifeboat Association, are the envy of the world; others, like the House of Lords, are the target of venegary [sic] politicians and music-hall comedians. Midway between the two, more sedate than the former and less democratic than the latter, lies the MCC.

LORD COBHAM, MCC treasurer, **1964**.

IT is perhaps seldom appreciated to what lengths the Committee of the MCC is prepared to go to achieve a right decision on some point of cricket lore.

LORD COBHAM.

DON'T take any notice of the damn committee.

HENRY PERKINS, retiring as MCC secretary, **1897**.

No human institution is perfect, but it would in my humble opinion, be impossible to find nicer men than those who constitute the government of Lord's.

SIR PELHAM WARNER, *Lord's 1787–1945*, **1946**.

THERE'S no more amateurish profession in the world. The sooner our counties get off their arses and do more for individuals the better.

JOHN EMBUREY, South African rebel tourist, **1989**.

I have been a member of the committee of the MCC and of the Conservative Cabinet and by comparison with the cricketers the Tories seemed like a bunch of Commies.

LORD MONCKTON at the MCC special meeting on South Africa, **1968**.

AT home and abroad in politics and sport, Britain will do better without the Tories and their friends of the Marylebone Cricket Club. Twenty years ago *Tribune* first made the demand that the MCC should be nationalised. Now everyone can see the wisdom of our policy.

MICHAEL FOOT in *Tribune*, after poor start to MCC's tour of Australia, **1958/9**.

IF there were a revolution in this country I'd now be in the first 10,000 to the guillotine, but not the first 1000.

JOHN WARR on being elected president of MCC in **1987**.

I had barely eaten my first meal on earth before my father wrote off to friends in England asking them to put my name down for MCC membership.

COLIN COWDREY, *MCC*, **1976**.

'What benefit is there to anyone, Middlesex or me, to stay here in that capacity?'
Phil Edmonds on leaving Leicester after being made 12th man by Middlesex.
Above, he felt differently when it was England

'His bowling is his mouthpiece. The only sound he (Richard Hadlee) ever makes on
the field is an excited yell – 'Howzaaatt' – whenever he is close to an lbw decision.
Often that is about three times an over.' Simon Hughes. *Below left*, Hadlee rejoices
in the 2nd Test, India *v* New Zealand, Bombay 1988

'Umpiring at the top now is full of comedians and gimmicks. In the old days there
used to be men you could respect.' Cec Pepper resigning from the umpire's list in
1980. *Below right*, David Shepherd gives his opinion

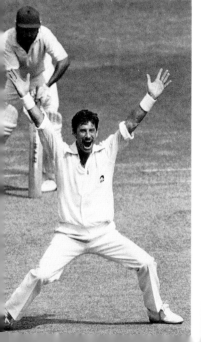

'It's not just wet, it's wet, wet.' Dickie Bird on the Headingley leak which swamped the bowlers' run up, 1987. *Above*, water hogs mop up the damage

'Terry got a great deal of lbws in this series, but most of them were taken with straight balls.' Bobby Simpson, Australia manager. *Below*, Chris Broad becomes one of Alderman's victims at Headingley, 1989

'Beer Cans Only in Seating Area. Glasses Prohibited.' Notice on the Long Room door leading to the member's terrace at Sydney, 1988. *Above left*, Australian appreciation of a good day's cricket

'I heard one Yorkshireman mutter, none too affectionately, "Here comes t'clown," as the blond-dyed hulk stepped out of his car wearing black leather trousers and a deckchair blazer. Later that day . . . he paraded his thigh-length cowboy boots before me. Between the two fashion shows he struck a magnificent 60.' Mike Brearley on Botham at the 1985 Headingley Test. *Above right*, Botham and his erstwhile agent Tim Hudson exhibit the deckchair blazers

'Our streaker was prettier than Twickenham's.' TCCB official after 19-year-old Sheila Nicholl's run at Lord's

'Unfortunately this has happened to someone who is not a very controversial character at all. Right through his career he has done nothing controversial and projects a good image of the game.' Micky Stewart on Chris Broad. *Above*, Broad knocks down his stumps after getting out in the Sydney Bicentennial Test, 1988

Below, Broad refuses to walk in the 'controversial' test series in Pakistan, 1987

SOME people talk about 'Botham' and 'Allott' as though they were discussing the labourers on the farm. I used to get angry as soon as I walked into Lord's.

IAN BOTHAM in *It Sort of Clicks*, Botham and Peter Roebuck, **1986**.

ONE of the absolutely unbreakable rules of cricket is that no one, but no one, disputes anything with the umpire, least of all the captain of England. There are no excuses.

OSSIE WHEATLEY, chairman of the TCCB cricket committee, justifying his veto over the reappointment of Mike Gatting as England captain following his row with Shakoor Rana, **1989**.

WE started the game. We have the moral right to lead it. If we let our standards slip, the others will slip too. It's up to us to impose draconian measures to make sure that doesn't happen.

OSSIE WHEATLEY.

AN old military man once said to me that any fool can run a dictatorship – it is the democracies that are difficult. Cricket is still the most democratic of sports.

OSSIE WHEATLEY, **1989**.

PROFESSIONAL sportsmen are hard people. Once you allow a chink to appear in the rules, they will drive a wedge through it.

OSSIE WHEATLEY.

IT would be unkind to David Gower to say he was clearly second choice or that the results would have been any different. While the England bowlers bowled as they did, it didn't matter who was captain. The result would have been the same four–nil stuffing.

OSSIE WHEATLEY, insisting that his veto had made no difference to the **1989** series *v* Australia.

THIS TCCB veto is ridiculous. There was so much stick flying around when England lost the Ashes that at least Ted Dexter and Micky Stewart should have been able to defend their own decisions. Things don't change very quickly. I remember going along to Lord's 20 years ago as captain, with four selectors, to choose the side to tour Australia. When we sat down there must have been 15 people around the table, all having their say.

RAY ILLINGWORTH on the Wheatley veto.

WE had to go out and field late in the day. I set no sort of example to the side, but I think they understood. I was miles away, wondering what on earth I had done to deserve suddenly being judged incapable. Nothing in life is sacred, but I do feel I had done enough to hang onto my place and my dignity.

DAVID GOWER on discovering that as well as losing the captaincy he had been left out of the West Indies touring party, **1989**.

I think it's only fair that the world should know that Ted and Micky wanted Gatting. They have taken a lot of stick and it's right that the record should be put straight.

OSSIE WHEATLEY, admitting in November that Dexter and Stewart had wanted to reappoint Mike Gatting as England captain in **1989**.

I maintain I can contribute more in one telephone discussion with the chairman, Ossie Wheatley, than all the amateurs in a hundred meetings on the subject of cricket.

TONY LEWIS, sacked from Glamorgan's cricket committee for non-attendance, **1980**.

THE Establishment seem to want my ability but not me.

GEOFFREY BOYCOTT, *In the Fast Lane*, **1981**.

YOU'VE got to get on with the powers that be, to tug the forelock.

PHIL EDMONDS, **1983**.

I will just do a bit of telepathy with Frances and see what she thinks.

PHIL EDMONDS' jibe on the *Wogan* show against a TCCB contract which forbade him to comment on the forthcoming England tour of Australia, **1986**. (Edmonds was summoned to Lord's to explain himself, but escaped with a ticking-off.)

THE visit to the dressing-room of a senior committee-man, watch-chain dangling, smacked of a Dickensian mill-owner's visit to a shop-floor. The players would stiffen into attitudes of modest respect. And if the committee-man's mien had a benevolent aspect, that was probably because he stood to lose nothing by the workmen's inefficiency.

MIKE BREARLEY on the Middlesex committee of the **1960s**, in *The Art of Captaincy*, **1985**.

MANY of your committee members are sitting there for no better reason than it is good for their business or social image to do so. They are status seekers who would as quickly get themselves on the tiddleywinks committee if that game should suddenly acquire prestige.

'BOMBER' WELLS, Gloucestershire spin bowler, **1970**.

I'M being paid half of what a mechanic gets for servicing my car – and I'm not complaining.

TED DEXTER, defending his £20,000-a-year salary as chairman of England cricket committee, **1989**.

ELLISON held a record which must be very hard to beat, viz., that he shot grouse on the first day of the grouse-shooting season for seventy successive years.

LORD HAWKE on his predecessor as Yorkshire president, M. J. Ellison, *Wisden*, **1932**.

COMMITTEE meeting held at the White Lion Hotel, Bristol, on Thursday, November 25th, at 3 o'clock. Present: E. M. Grace, and that's all.

MINUTES of a Gloucestershire committee meeting. (E.M. was secretary from **1870** to **1909**.)

THE captains and committees of the sixties will have a lot to answer for in the course of time. They are making a drudgery of a beautiful game.

JOHN WOODCOCK, *The Times*, **1966**.

I have the greatest affection for the county of my birth, but for the committee as a body, the greatest contempt.

W. G. GRACE, resigning as Gloucestershire captain, **1899**.

THEY'VE done the hat-trick on us, uncle.

DAVID GRAVENEY to Tom Graveney after being deposed as Gloucestershire captain in **1988**. Tom had been replaced by a young Old Etonian, Tom Pugh, in 1960, and his brother Ken was deposed as county chairman.

MAY I congratulate you on having buggered the career of another young cricketer.

LORD DEERHURST, president of Worcestershire, to Lord Harris in the Long Room at Lord's **1922**. Harris had succeeded in banning Walter Hammond from county cricket for rest of season after his defection from Kent to Gloucestershire.

IT was decided that on account of the heavy expenses already incurred with next year's ground staff, an engagement could not be offered W. Rhodes of Huddersfield.

WARWICKSHIRE COMMITTEE MINUTES, **1897**.

I thought things were changing with people like Gatting and Botham leading their counties. But Hampshire obviously still prefer public schoolboys. Perhaps I don't have enough initials – it's a handicap having only two.

TREVOR JESTY, leaving Hampshire for Surrey after being passed over for captaincy, **1985**.

YOU do have a private income, don't you?

MIDDLESEX COMMITTEE MEN to Mike Brearley on his appointment as captain.

THE Chairman of the cricket committee would come into the dressing-room just before we were going out to play an important Gillette Cup match and start telling us how the Sussex Martlets had got on on Sunday. And he expected us to be interested.

JOHN SNOW.

Sussex have always been regarded as the amateur gin-and-tonic men of English cricket – well, I'm going to change all that.

TONY GREIG, Sussex captain, **1974**.

HELLO Ken, I've been meaning to have a word with you. How's the wife and family? All right I hope. Oh, by the way, you're not being re-engaged for next season.

EDDIE HARRISON, chairman of Sussex's cricket committee, informing Ken Suttle in the Hove car park that he was not receiving a new contract, **1970**. (Quoted in John Snow's *Cricket Rebel*, 1976.)

As we took our seats, he looked across at Tony Greig and said: 'Ah, you must be Greig because you're so tall.' Then he turned to me and said: 'I recognize you because I've seen your picture in the newspapers;' and finally he came to Ken Suttle and said: 'That means you must be Ken Suttle because the three of you were coming.'

JOHN SNOW on a Sussex committee man meeting the three at a winter cricket dinner after Suttle had completed a run of 423 consecutive appearances for the county.

WHO was that man I've been talking to?

ENGLAND SELECTOR to Bob Willis. It was Phil Edmonds.

GOOD morning Roy, good morning Peter.

ALEC BEDSER, chairman of England selectors, greeting Ray East and John Lever in lift during Test trial, **1973**.

IT's unbelievable, but it's the old bowler hat and the umbrella and the 'Morning Illingworth' – they're still back in the thirties, they really are.

RAY ILLINGWORTH, then at Leicestershire, on Yorkshire committee, **1973**.

WHEN I left Yorkshire I received a letter from the secretary saying they were not going to offer me a contract which began: 'Dear Ray Illingworth', but the 'Ray' had been crossed out. They couldn't even bring themselves to call me by my first name or use a fresh piece of paper.

RAY ILLINGWORTH.

HE said some silly things like 'Of course when the team manager is checking the hotel bills, we would want you to give a hand with the luggage.'

> RAY ILLINGWORTH's version of his meeting with Doug Insole to discuss the role of the English cricket manager. Illingworth turned down the job. (From *The Tempestuous Years*, **1987**).

I would rather the Australians won 2–1 or 3–1 than go through the dismal business of four more draws.

> DAVID CLARK, MCC manager in Australia, after first two Tests were drawn, **1970/71** tour. The captain, Illingworth, did not agree.

MR Bloody Warner will go to bed when I've finished with him.

> CHARLIE PARKER, Gloucestershire's left-arm spin bowler, after a public scuffle with Pelham Warner, whom he partly blamed for his lack of Test caps, **1929**.

I'VE always thought the selectors were a bunch of idiots. All they've done now is confirm it.

> JEFF THOMSON, omitted from Australian tour party to England, **1981**.

MY God, look what they've sent me.

> A. C. MACLAREN on the team selected for England *v* Australia, Fourth Test, Old Trafford, **1902**. The selectors had left out Fry, Jessop and Barnes.

THE selectors wanted to see Tate bowl on a wet wicket, and so they should.

> A. C. MACLAREN's explanation for leaving out Hirst, who was in the twelve in that match. MacLaren and Lord Hawke, the chairman of the selectors, had been sparring throughout the season.

WE didn't want to go overboard, although changes had to be made.

> PETER MAY making six changes for the Leeds Test *v* West Indies in **1988**, including Chris Cowdrey as the third captain of the series.

I may not be a good enough player, or have the right leadership qualities, but at least I deserve an explanation of where I went wrong.

> CHRIS COWDREY after being dropped as captain after only one Test *v* West Indies, **1988**.

IT's about time some big, big men started being honest with themselves.

> VIV RICHARDS, pointing at England's cricket management as the source of England's woes after Cowdrey's Test, Headingley, **1988**.

I was absolutely numbed when I heard the names. It's about the worst selection I've ever known. There has been so much disquiet about recent selection policy, we must do something about it.

> JACKIE COURT, former England batsman, on the 22 players selected for the Test trial by England's women selectors, **1988**.

I'M not suggesting favouritism, just poor judgement.

> MEGAN LEAR, England international, on the same selections, **1988**.

I think they must be mad.

> PHIL EDMONDS, on being omitted by Middlesex so they could play four seamers at Leicester, two days after he had helped England win the Ashes.

WHAT benefit is there to anyone, Middlesex or me, to stay here in that capacity?

> PHIL EDMONDS, on leaving Leicester after being made twelfth man by Middlesex.

As far as cricket is concerned, Butcher is English now.

> ALEC BEDSER, naming West Indian Roland Butcher in the England party for the **1981** tour of the Caribbean.

FROM the humanitarian point of view, why should a cricketer born in Papua New Guinea, Zimbabwe, Israel or one of the other associate countries be denied the opportunity of a Test career by an accident of birth?

ALAN SMITH, chief executive TCCB, arguing for a reduction in the qualifying period for Graeme Hick in **1988**.

WE don't make certain that a doctor is present and we don't intend to. Several doctors are keen followers of cricket and there are usually some present. There are always cars to take anyone to hospital if necessary.

MAJOR DOUGLAS CARR, of Derbyshire, in the wake of kiss-of-life needed by Glamorgan's Roger Davis when struck in close-fielding position, Glamorgan v Warwickshire at Cardiff, **1971**.

THE Queen is not a great cricket fan, but she knew the English team were struggling a bit.

MIKE GATTING on receiving the OBE, **1988**.

I'M not aware of any mistakes I've made this summer.

TED DEXTER, after disastrous England Ashes summer, **1989**.

9
Those Hallowed Turfs

Grounds

Lord's

SIR – Now I know that this country is finished. On Saturday, with Australia playing, I asked a London cabby to take me to Lord's and had to show him the way.

LETTER to *The Times*.

AFTER all, Lord's is Lord's.

LORD'S ATTENDANT, requesting men to replace their shirts after complaints from women members, Middlesex *v* Yorkshire, **1959**.

SIR – I noticed one of the umpires today disgraced Lord's Ground by appearing with bicycle clips round his trousers during his work, surely rather infra-dig for the World's premier cricket ground.

LETTER to the secretary, MCC, posted up in Lord's Pavilion, **1923**.

THOSE in control at Lord's should remember that but for such men as these the historic enclosure might now be a German beer garden.

THE CRICKETER editorial on the refusal of admission to disabled soldiers because their chairs took up too much space, England *v* Australia, **1921**.

AUSTRALIANS will always fight for those 22 yards. Lord's and its traditions belong to Australia just as much as to England.

JOHN CURTIN, Australian Prime Minister, towards end of Second World War, **1945**.

EXPECT every ball to shoot and you will be in time if she rises; if watching too eagerly for the rise you will be too late if she shoots.

ADVICE to batsmen playing at Lord's in the **1820s/30s**.

My immediate reaction was: 'How on earth can major cricket be played on this?'

JIM FAIRBROTHER, Lord's groundsman, on his first sight of the slope, in *Testing the Wicket*, **1985**.

I shudder at the cold gloomy picture of Lord's or Melbourne 'Bull Ring' after play is ended. The man who wrote 'The song is ended but the melody lingers on' never, I'll warrant, played cricket on either of these grounds.

ARTHUR MAILEY.

Derby

MORE reported cases of frostbite than any other first-class venue.

JON AGNEW, *8 Days A Week*, **1988**.

Ebbw Vale

WHEN I tap the pitch with my bat, someone else taps back.

PETER WALKER, of Glamorgan, on Ebbw Vale wicket, **1967**.

Hambledon

How those brawn-faced fellows of farmers would drink to our success! And then what stuff they had to drink! Punch! Not your new Ponche à la Romaine or Ponche à la Groseille, or your modern cat-lap milk punch – punch – punch be-deviled. But good, unsophisticated John Bull stuff – stark! – that would stand on end – punch that would make a cat speak!

JOHN NYREN, recalling cricket at Hambledon in the **1780s**.

I really wanted to see Hambledon, and had built up a romantic picture of what it should be like. We got there one afternoon, and searched the village for the ground. Eventually I found it. . . . No charming village green, no church, just rather a bleak stretch of ground opposite the old pub. It was one of my great disappointments.

BOB TAYLOR, **1982**.

Headingley

THERE'S a bastard in my family and it's sitting out there.

KEITH BOYCE, Headingley groundsman, on his Test wicket, **1985**.

THERE wasn't time to think of timeless Tests at Leeds.

DON BRADMAN, *Wisden*, **1939**.

I'd throw them off the top of the pavilion. Mind, I'm a fair man, I'd give them a 50–50 chance. I'd have Keith Fletcher underneath trying to catch them.

FRED TRUEMAN on the saboteurs of the Test wicket, **1975**.

Hove

IT is a genial mixture of the raffish and run-down, like the numerous blazers in the pavilion bar, most sporting military buttons and yet many with frayed cuffs.

GEORGE PLUMPTRE, *Homes of Cricket*, **1988**.

Kent grounds

ONE sees more pretty cricket in Kent in a three-day match than can be seen anywhere else in England in a fortnight.

LEARIE CONSTANTINE, *Cricket in the Sun*.

Melbourne

AFTER two overs at Melbourne there are practically no outside stitches, no glossy appearance, on the ball.

MAURICE TATE.

Old Trafford

THERE was a time when the weather was not responsible for some very awkward wickets at Old Trafford, at a time too when Walter Brearley was our fast bowler, which made some of our opponents wonder once or twice if our wickets were kept rough on purpose.

A. C. MACLAREN.

WHEN my innings had not lasted more than twenty minutes, I managed in that short time to collect a full pocket of pebbles, which I bounced on the Committee room table on my way up to the dressing-room, informing our members of the true reason for our low scores.

A. C. MACLAREN on the Lancashire Committee's criticism of the team's low scores in the **1880s**.

I suppose if you don't play in gloom up here you never play at all.

ALAN KNOTT, **1981**.

Scarborough

FIRST-CLASS cricket on holiday.

J. M. KILBURN.

SOMEONE asked me if it was true that I had hit a ball into Trafalgar Square and was it hit from Lord's or The Oval. When I said it was Trafalgar Square, Scarborough . . . he wasn't so much impressed.

C. I. 'BUNS' THORNTON on his six off A. G. Steel, **1887**.

I'D like to build a row of houses right across this wicket. Any more tricks like this and I'll be finished in 12 months.

FRED TRUEMAN after Warwickshire had scored 269 *v* Yorkshire, **1963**.

Sheffield

FRED Trueman's forever moaning about this wicket; but it's only an 'abit. 'E knows Wilfred's taken five wickets on 'ere and scored sixty odd, same day.

TOM PARKIN, groundsman at Bramall Lane.

Swansea

From the top of the hill top pavilion.
The sea is a cheat to the eye.
Where it secretly seeps into coastline,
Or fades in the yellow-grey sky;
But the crease marks are sharp on the green,
As the axe's first taste of the tree,
And keen is the Welshman's assault,
As the freshening fret from the sea.

JOHN ARLOTT, opening lines of *Cricket at Swansea*.

Sydney

THE Hill at Sydney used to be amusing, sharp and cutting, but not unfriendly; now it's simply foul-mouthed and crude.

GEOFFREY BOYCOTT, **1979**.

I enjoyed it, but if I go back again I'll wear a tin hat.

LAURIE LEE, poet and author, knocked unconscious by a beer bottle on Sydney Hill, watching Australia *v* New Zealand, **1974**.

THE latest news is that the Hill at Sydney is to be replaced by a stand, so much the better.

E. W. SWANTON, *Follow On*, **1977**.

BEER Cans Only in Seating Area. Glasses Prohibited.

NOTICE on the Long Room door leading to the Members' terrace at Sydney pavilion, **1988**.

Taunton

OUR spectators went barmy, flung their hats in the air and hit each other about. And they varmers do talk about it to this day.

SAMMY WOODS on Somerset's last-ball victory over Surrey at Taunton, **1891**, their first in first-class cricket.

I make the crowd 24; 23 really, because one of them's died there overnight.

TOM YOUNG to R. C. Robertson-Glasgow during a Somerset match at Taunton in the **1920s**.

STEADY boys, best put down a canary first.

J. B. EVANS, Glamorgan fast bowler, about to descend into visitors' basement dressing-room at Taunton.

The Oval

THE sun always seemed to burn from a cloudless sky at The Oval, dark blue except where it was streaked by the white trail of a passing jet.

CHRISTOPHER MARTIN-JENKINS in his Introduction to the *Wisden Book of County Cricket*.

AT The Oval, men seem to have rushed away with some zest from their City offices. At Lord's there is a dilettante look, as of men whose work, if any, has yet to come.

REV. JAMES PYCROFT, *Oxford Memories*, **1886**.

WHERE's the groundsman's hut? If I had a rifle I'd shoot him now.

BILL O'REILLY, Australian spin bowler, during England's 903–7, **1938**.

The WACA, Perth

You have to clap yourself on at the WACA.

GARY GILMOUR, on the parochialism of Perth crowds.

Trent Bridge

I grew up here in the fifties, and spent half my time watching people nod off and go home early. Just lately they bloody well haven't. The last ten years have been terrifically exciting here.

RON ALLSOPP, Nottinghamshire groundsman, answering criticisms of the club's wickets, **1988**.

A lotus-land for batsmen, a place where it was always afternoon and 360 for 2 wickets.

NEVILLE CARDUS.

Worcester

Look at that, Parkin, 32 overs, 8 maidens, 92 runs, 1 wicket. And they send missionaries to China!

CECIL PARKIN, Lancashire spin bowler, suffering a flat wicket in late **1920s**.

If those boat people want a job, they can come and bowl on this bloody wicket.

NORMAN GIFFORD, Worcestershire spinner, with similar troubles 50 years later, **1978**.

Crowds

It's been a reasonable day for us boozers up here in private boxes. But what about the geezers queueing and those blokes munching their sandwiches up there at the Nursery End?

MICK JAGGER, after Saturday's play in the **1980** Centenary Test at Lord's between England and Australia was abandoned because of a wet ground.

OFFICIAL hospitality is an organized conspiracy to prevent the uninterrupted watching of cricket, based upon a constant invitation to 'have a drink' or 'meet our sales manager from Slough'.

ROY HATTERSLEY, Labour MP, in the *Guardian*, **1983**.

IN a pub, worse than the 'buttonholer' is the 'expert'. There's a terribly self-satisfied little jerk in the Coach and Horses – he calls himself an advertising executive, whatever that means – who was telling us the other day that Botham doesn't hold his bat correctly. He then addressed Mr Botham himself on the television screen and told him to adjust his left hand. He has even given Mr Piggott riding instructions.

JEFFREY BERNARD.

THE one thing that strikes me about the average crowd – and this is more true of the South than the North – is its ignorance, its startling and fathomless ignorance, of the game in general and the match that is going on in particular.

DUDLEY CAREW, *The Cricketer*, **1928**.

IT is to be feared that a good many people who find their pleasure in watching cricket are very ignorant of the game. In no other way can one account for the unseemly 'barracking' that sometimes goes on.

SYDNEY PARDON, editor, *Wisden*, **1919**.

AT about two o'clock the sun came out and a great crowd assembled outside the ground. What I hadn't thought of was that two umpires and two captains would sit and wait for so long without making a decision. The crowd broke in, and to save our skins we started to play at 5.20 on a swamp.

ROBERT RYDER, Edgbaston administrator, on England *v* Australia, **1902**.

To call a crowd 'a crowd' in Jamaica is a misnomer. It should be called a mob . . . these people still belong to the jungles and forests instead of a civilised society.

SUNIL GAVASKAR, on India's **1976** tour of West Indies, in *Sunny Days*.

No sir. Ah didn't coom here t'quell riot. Ah coom t'play cricket.

TED PEATE, refusing Surrey official's request to help stem crowd riot, with England needing only 11 runs to win, *v* Australia, **1884**.

No, we'll stay. We want another wicket or two this evening.

LEN HUTTON, refusing to leave field for fear of crowd riot, Guyana, MCC tour of West Indies, **1953/4**.

I've seen people hit by bottles and it makes a bloody mess of them.

RAY ILLINGWORTH, England captain, defending decision to take players off the field during crowd trouble at Sydney, **1971**.

STOP the game. We can't see the game. Smoke is getting in our eyes.

G. K. MENON, Indian reporter, striding on to Bombay outfield from press box as stands were set alight, India *v* Australia, **1969**.

ONE problem was that gentlemen with white and brown faces confronted each other quite determined to have a punch-up. I have never seen it before on a Test ground.

RAMAN SUBBA ROW, TCCB chairman, after crowd trouble during England *v* Pakistan one-day international at Edgbaston, **1987**.

ONE of the main problems is too much drink.

IAN BOTHAM, reacting to the same Edgbaston crowd trouble, **1987**.

I may be black, but I know who my parents are.

VIV RICHARDS, jumping into the crowd at Weston to confront some racist hecklers.

ON Sundays in particular, we are subjected to the moronic chanting beloved of soccer crowds and decent folk are being driven away by the kind of mindless exhibitionism that has dogged football.

BOB TAYLOR describing dangers of one-day cricket, in *Standing Up, Standing Back*, **1985**.

WE have got a freaker [sic] down the wicket now, not very shapely as it is masculine and I would think it has seen the last of its cricket for the day. The police are mustered, so are the cameramen and Greg Chappell. No! He has had his load, he is being embraced by a blond policeman and this may be his last public appearance. But what a splendid one. And so warm!

JOHN ARLOTT's BBC radio commentary, Lord's Test v Australia, **1975**. For 'freaker' read cricket's first 'streaker'. (From *The Ashes: Highlights since 1948*, **1989**.)

I'M this side of the line, you're that side and never the twain shall meet. If they do I'll break your – teeth.

RODNEY MARSH, Australian wicket-keeper, to a spectator who fielded a ball inside the boundary rope, **1981**.

A limit to youthful enthusiasm is reached when those delightful young rascals career over the playing area after scalps.

THE CRICKETER comment on the depredations of autograph hunters at Lord's, Middlesex v Sussex, **1921**.

WE must be the only working-class family in Western Australia who have gone ex-directory.

BILL DONNISON, whose son, Gary, was rugby tackled by Australia's Terry Alderman when he invaded the pitch, causing Alderman to damage a shoulder, **1983**.

OWING to the pitch being deliberately torn up by the public, I, as captain of the Lancashire eleven, cannot see my way to continue the game, the groundsman bearing me out that the wicket could not again be put right.

A. C. MACLAREN, statement to press, **1907**. MacLaren refused to play on in Middlesex v Lancashire match at Lord's after a few spectators walked across the pitch.

IT serves thee right. Tha should bowl at bloody wickets.

NELSON SUPPORTER to Ray Lindwall, Australian quickie, when his debut was marred by dropped slip catches.

BAILEY, I wish you was a statue and I was a pigeon.

SYDNEY HILLITE, **1954/5** tour of Australia.

COME on Brearley, for God's sake; you make Denness look like Don Bradman.

MELBOURNE BARRACKER, Australia *v* England, **1978/9**.

GOLD Medallion Award for Greatest Winger Would Have To Be Won By J. M. Brearley, Classical Music Lover.

BANNER at Melbourne Cricket Ground, England's **1979/80** tour.

IT'S so depressing out here. Shout something encouraging, you chaps!

PHIL EDMONDS to the Oval crowd as Pakistan scored 708 in the Fifth Test, **1987**.

THIS could be your last Test.

A SPECTATOR'S response to Edmonds' request.

WHEN you dream, as I did last night, that you've been picked to open the batting for MCC in Australia and come the great day you can't find your bat, you don't really need Freud or the Maudsley Hospital to give you clues as to the balance in your mental account.

JEFFREY BERNARD, **1982**.

THE drums. I miss the drums.

VIV RICHARDS after the TCCB decision to ban musical instruments, hooters etc. at Test matches, **1988**.

10
They Also Serve

Umpires

WHEN you play in a match, be sure not to forget to pay a little attention to the umpire. First of all enquire after his health, then say what a fine player his father was, and, finally, present him with a brace of birds or rabbits. This will give you confidence, and you will probably do well.

GEORGE PARR (as told by Edward Lucas).

AN umpire should be a man. They are, for the most part, old women.

ROBERT FITZGERALD, *Jerks from Short Leg*, **1866**.

MANY umpires are now too old, and their sight not good enough.

SIR HOME GORDON, *The Cricketer*, **1821**.

Now all you want is a white stick.

SYDNEY BARNES, handing a stray dog he had captured to umpire Alex Skelding in **1948**. (Barnes' caustic wit arose from a refused lbw appeal.)

UMPIRING at the top now is full of comedians and gimmicks. In the old days there used to be men you could respect.

CEC PEPPER, resigning from first-class umpire's list, **1980**.

WE have far too much to do in the game these days. You need one eye up your backside.

ARTHUR JEPSON, umpire, bemoaning arrival of fielding circles in one-day cricket, **1981**.

THEY are the only people out there in my age group.

JACK SIMMONS, explaining why he spent so much time chatting to umpires during overs, **1985**.

WHAT goes on in the middle is our business, nothing to do with anybody else.

MERVYN KITCHEN replying to press questions about no-balling Jeff Thomson, **1985**.

IN Bombay when England batting there are forty to fifty thousand people shouting every time ball hitting the pad, and in Calcutta, my God, there are ninety thousand people all shouting. But you must concentrate. It is a selfish thing but you must concentrate to save your skin.

SWAROOP KISHEN, Indian Test umpire, in Scyld Berry's *Cricket Wallah*, **1982**.

THE modern umpire is caught between two opposing forces – the domestic pressures which encourage error, and the technology which reveals them.

IMRAN KHAN, *All Round View*, **1988**.

DOUBT? When I'm umpiring, there's never any doubt!

FRANK CHESTER, asked when he gave a batsman the benefit of the doubt.

UMPIRE cursing is previous to Hambledon. Umpire-defiance is older than Dr Grace. He is but a weak-kneed cricketer who *in his heart* approves of the umpire's decisions.

R. C. ROBERTSON-GLASGOW.

THE only acceptable form of dissent is a dirty look. And we don't like that.

England Test umpire. **1982**.

I don't understand why, in a democratic society, where government and all the accepted standards in every walk of life are being questioned, umpires should be immune.

ASIF IQBAL, Kent captain, **1982**.

YOU must be a rogue or a fool.
I suppose I'm a little of both sir.

EXCHANGE between Sir Timothy O'Brien and the umpire at a Cambridgeshire country house match after the former had been given out caught off his shoulder. According to 'Buns' Thornton, the above version has three expletives deleted.

I couldn't see why I should stand there and have players looking at me as if I were a leper.

TOM BROOKS, retiring as umpire during Australia v England series, **1978/9**.

IF they won't accept decisions, there is no point carrying on. Why should I? I'm nearly 60. I don't have to live with this kind of pressure.

ARTHUR FAGG, Test umpire, after West Indies' Rohan Kanhai showed dissent, England v West Indies at Edgbaston, **1973**.

I'M sorry about that decision, Mr Allen, but I had to get to the gents'.

UMPIRE BESTWICK to Gubby Allen, after adjudging Denis Compton lbw on his Middlesex debut, **1936**.

AMATEUR players would rather sweep roads or sell newspapers in the street than pretend to be first-class umpires.

CROSS-ARROW, *The Cricketer*, **1927**.

I'VE always had to count the pennies.

SYD BULLER on an umpire's lot, **1965**.

I have nightmares about having to become an umpire.

JOHN SNOW giving evidence in the High Court on the Packer affair, **1978**.

IT's not easy taking up umpiring after being an umpire baiter for over 30 years.

BILL ALLEY, on joining umpires list, **1969**.

MOST umpires have good memories. If you stuff them once, they'll stuff you good and proper in the end.

ALAN OAKMAN, Warwickshire coach, *From the Nursery End*, **1985**.

SEE those bloody vultures up there. They're waiting for that bloody umpire. He's got to be dead.

SAM LOXTON, Australian manager, to Pakistan army representatives, when Hanif was given 'not out' against Lindwall in Dacca Test.

YOU'LL never die wondering, son.

CEC PEPPER, umpire, reacting to numerous lbw appeals from Ashley Mallett, Australian spin bowler, **1968**.

As God is my witness!

ALEX SKELDING, umpire, awarding a hat-trick of lbw decisions to Yorkshire's Horace Fisher *v* Somerset at Scarborough, **1932**.

HE's out and we've won the Championship!

UMPIRE AND WELSHMAN DAI DAVIES, giving decision as John Clay took wicket which gave Glamorgan their first County Championship success, **1948**.

HE'D better not bite that – it's the finger I give 'em all out with.

DICKIE BIRD, attacked by Billy, an Amazon parrot from Aylesbury, while judging the annual talking bird contest, NEC, Birmingham, **1989**.

THE 'Outer' – large of frame, rubicund of countenance, who drinks pints and eats vastly, is a gay, carefree fellow who, in his playing days, was a fast bowler and who now has only to hear somebody in the crowd clear his throat for his finger to shoot aloft.

MICHAEL STEVENSON in *The Cricketer*, **1963**.

THE 'Not Outer' . . . is small, wizened, misanthropic, drinks half-shandies and eats sparingly.

MICHAEL STEVENSON, as above.

BATSMEN seem to be getting away with lbw appeals which make me wonder about the umpires. It would be only human, if every critical decision is to be played back endlessly, for them to opt for less controversy and aggravation. I pray that our umpires are not becoming 'Not Outers'.

SIR LEN HUTTON on the effect of TV coverage in **1985**, England *v* Australia series.

DEREK Underwood could never bowl at my end – he could not get round me.

SWAROOP KISHEN, heavyweight Indian Test umpire, admission to Dickie Bird. (From *That's Out*, **1985**.)

OSLEAR found something in the rules to get off the pitch because of cold last year, but I can't find the bloody thing.

DICKIE BIRD, umpiring at Derby, (*8 Days a Week*, Jon Agnew **1988**.)

IT's not just wet, it's wet wet.

DICKIE BIRD as play was delayed in the Headingley Test because of a blocked drain, **1988**.

HERE's three ha'pence. Buy a paper and find out the score.

> ALEX SKELDING, umpire, at odds with scoreboard operators in a county match.

Sponsors, Scorers, Groundsmen, Gatemen

SPONSORS are sponsors and if they become too powerful we could finish up in a situation where the sponsors are making the decisions.

> CHRIS PEAKER, Lancashire CCC treasurer, recommending an increase in subscriptions as a way of members safeguarding their control in **1988**. The attempt was rejected.

I know of no other business that would secretly negotiate such a deal without bothering to inform its sponsor.

> LEN OWEN, Benson and Hedges special events manager, on the TCCB's decision to award television rights for the B&H Cup in 1990 to British Satellite Broadcasting. The sponsors were told less than 24 hours before the deal was made public, **1989**.

WHEN you come as a sponsor you are treated like royalty. I'd recommend it to anyone. When you come as a member on Test-match Saturday you are shunted around as some species of sub-human.

> DOUGLAS LEVER, Lancashire member and sponsor, on differing approaches at Old Trafford, **1988**.

AT last year's B&H final hundreds [of paying spectators] were turned away, yet the boxes were brimming with the uninitiated. In one a man with a large whisky asked me animatedly, 'By the way, do you still have sixes in cricket?'

> SIMON HUGHES, Middlesex seam bowler, on the spread of sponsorship, **1988**.

THERE was a social prejudice against the scorer who was a descendant of the baggage man.

> VIC ISAACS, Hampshire scorer and statistician, quoted in *A Walk to the Wicket* by Ted Dexter and David Lemmon, **1985**.

THE scientists fail us . . . they cannot do anything to supply men who are born to be groundsmen.

COLIN COWDREY, *MCC*, **1976**.

IT is a remarkable fact that every time a side has a bad innings it is the wicket that is blamed – never the player.

THE GROUNDSMAN, **1958**.

THANK God Nasser has taken over the Suez Canal. Otherwise, I'd have been plastered over every front page like Marilyn Monroe.

BERT FLACK, Old Trafford groundsman, after Laker's 19 wickets for England against Australia, **1956**.

THEY'VE got it easy. They operate in the growing season.

STAN GIBSON, Manchester City groundsman, on his cricketing opposite numbers, **1989**.

THERE should have been a last line of defence during the war. It would have been made up entirely of the more officious breed of cricket stewards. If Hitler had tried to invade these shores he would have been met by a short, stout man in a white coat who would have said: 'I don't care who you are, you're not coming in here unless you're a member.'

RAY EAST in *A Funny Turn*, **1983**.

I didn't know he was the England captain, and he didn't tell me. I'm afraid I don't follow cricket; boxing's my game.

HEADINGLEY GATEMAN who refused Chris Cowdrey admission to the ground the day before the Fourth Test *v* West Indies, **1988**.

The Media

WHY should I buy cricket? Nobody watches it.

GREG DYKE, chairman of the ITV Network Sports Committee, **1988**.

. . . and the press box creaking, stretching,
fidgeting, vulture-like waits
with the sound of sharpening carbon claws
for the fresh carcass of play.

JOHN SNOW, from Lord's Test, in *Moments and Thoughts*, **1973**.

JOURNALISM and batting are not so different . . . a few good strokes
are often better remembered than all the padding in between.

TED DEXTER, **1974**.

BRITISH AIRWAYS STEWARD: Would you like me to take anything
home for you?
BOB WILLIS: Yes, 34 journalists and two camera crews.

ENGLAND'S tour of West Indies, **1986**.

ENGLISH first-class cricket has been played for the benefit of the
cricket writers and the newspapers . . . most writers know the
parlous state of county cricket, yet they had to support it, to ensure
it survived to support them. They had a vested interest in the system
which existed.

ANDREW CARO, former WSC managing director, on press's hostile reaction to
Packer Circus, *Wisden Cricket Monthly*, **1980**.

I will never be accepted by the snob press.

RAY ILLINGWORTH, **1973**.

THE press wanted my reaction to the Yorkshire decision and when I
refused to comment . . . they did what the press usually do. They
became cutting and critical, as if it was my job to fill their columns
for them. They smile and then they stab – and they think the next
time they come along for a comment you are going to forget the
wounding things they write and obligingly talk to them.

GEOFFREY BOYCOTT on his sacking as Yorkshire captain, in *Put to the Test*, **1979**.

DURING these tours the captain is interviewed by reporters more or less all day, sometimes early in the morning when I was in my bath. It is policy to receive them even with a bath towel, because if you don't, they will report you just the same, only it would be their idea of things, not mine.

E. J. METCALFE, describing Colonel Greenway's tour to Philadelphia, 1913, in *The Cricketer*, 1932.

I knew I could never be a 'real' newspaper journalist – it was such a difficult job to be hail-fellow-well-met-what's-yours-old-boy in private life and next day have to scalpel-slash a reputation in public print.

FRANK KEATING, *Another Bloody Day in Paradise*, 1981.

I do know that I wouldn't enjoy making my living by criticising my former colleagues.

BOB WILLIS, 1983.

I have grown to trust and like several of the cricket writers. Equally, there are some I trust but don't like, others I like but don't trust and the occasional individual I neither like nor trust.

BOB WILLIS, *The Captain's Diary*, 1983.

WHEN you have to spend the tour in your hotel room so you're not stitched up, there's something wrong.

IAN BOTHAM, England's tour of West Indies, 1986.

ONE would suppose that the invasion of publicity and the general mateyness of radio and press would have tended to produce something like swollen-headedness in the prominent players. But one would be in error. The tendency, so far as one can see, is for publicity to produce more and more modesty of demeanour.

C. B. FRY, *The Cricketer*, 1955.

IT may be hoped that the MCC will in future remove their edict, which does not permit a cricketer on tour abroad to write on that tour, and appoint one of the team, who can be trusted not to commit faux pas, to write descriptions of the matches.

THE CRICKETER on lack of news of West Indies tour, **1926**.

MY ghost is writing rubbish.

ENGLAND PLAYER on West Indies tour, **1986**.

THESE experts are spoiling the market for the others. They are no journalists – the mere writing of articles does not make one a journalist. You have to go through the mill, then develop specialisation. Anyway, no cricketer I have ever known was able to write well.

ALEX BANNISTER, *Daily Mail* correspondent.

ONE gets used to the abysmal ignorance of some colleagues, to whom any slip catch has resulted from 'an outswinger' and any shot which ends in the third man area is 'a cut'.

MIKE STEVENSON, returning to teaching, on his erstwhile colleagues in the press box, **1982**.

JUDGEMENTS by commentators should be made on probability, not outcome. So when Jim Laker writes in the *Express* on Friday that it was a mistake to put Australia in to bat at The Oval, one should know that his opinion (given to Paul Parker's father) an hour before the start on Thursday was that we should field. And it is facile to refer to playing only four specialist bowlers as 'folly' only after three of them have broken down.

MIKE BREARLEY, **1981**.

IT's plastic-cupped, can-I-borrow-your-phone press boxes. When we talk it's talk of mortgages. 'Whose turn, old boy?' means 'Get out your Thermos.' You can never borrow a Biro, they've only got fountain pens. When play gets going, it's eyes down into *Wisden*.

FRANK KEATING on life in cricket press boxes, **1974**.

By 2000 the TV camera will be everywhere: dressing room, hotel and bathroom. I visualise the newsman's mania for live human action and reaction breaking all the bounds of privacy and decency.

TONY LEWIS, 1969.

THE BBC did not apologise to viewers who were deprived of seeing half of Botham's century on Saturday at Old Trafford because somebody in his wisdom decided precedence should be taken by a horserace from Newbury and the Midland Bank Horse Trials.

RICHARD INGRAMS, 1981.

WE weren't at all impressed by their World Cup coverage. They failed to appreciate the significance of the Cup, and when we went to play a Test series in Pakistan afterwards the only coverage was in news bulletins.

PETER LUSH, England tour manager, on the BBC as the special relationship began to break down, 1988.

ONE viewer told me the other day that listening to my old mate Jim Laker and his new sidekick Bob Willis was better than taking two Mogadon.

FRED TRUEMAN on TV commentators, 1985.

IF anybody had told me I was one day destined to make a reputation as a writer on cricket I should have felt hurt.

NEVILLE CARDUS, *Autobiography*, 1947.

AH reckon, Mr Cardus, tha's invented me.

EMMOTT ROBINSON.

AH'D like to bowl at bugger soom da-ay.

DICK TYLDESLEY, Lancashire batsman, about Neville Cardus. (Quoted in Cardus's *Autobiography*, 1947.)

IT is doubtful whether anyone, unwittingly, has done more harm to the game than Cardus. No doubt unconsciously, Cardus condescended to cricket, encapsulating social attitudes that were unreal even when he started watching it. Cricket writers deal in stereotypes, stereotypes with regional and social overtones – Ranji, the wily Oriental, Tyldesley the honest yeoman, MacLaren, the lordly aristo. On the one hand the gents, on the other, lovable but inarticulate, full of character and simple humour, possessed of a God-given gift they did not rightly understand – the professionals.

NICHOLAS RICHARDSON, *New Society*, **1975**.

BUT my dear chap, it's the spirit of the thing that counts. Often when I quoted a player he may not literally have said those things. But he'd have liked to.

NEVILLE CARDUS.

JOHN ARLOTT has been that rarity, a man respected by the players as much as the public . . . somehow Arlott's presence made you feel cricket was in good hands.

BRIAN BRAIN, *Another Day, Another Match*, **1981**.

IT's one thing to do commentary and then go and write your newspaper report, but then it's altogether a different thing when at ten to seven you go out with 250 miles to drive home.

JOHN ARLOTT, explaining reasons for his retirement, BBC Radio, **1980**.

WELL, there's only one thing I can say after that over, and that's to clap my hands.

TREVOR BAILEY.

GOSH, it's difficult to identify these chaps. Sometimes they turn out to be brothers or cousins, and sometimes not to be related at all.

HENRY BLOFELD, coming to terms with Pakistan tourists, **1987**. (Source: Frank Keating, the *Guardian*.)

11
Showing the Flag

Touring

UP, breakfast, stretch, practice, play, bathe, bar, steak, bed. Same company, day in, day out.

IAN BOTHAM on touring in *It Sort of Clicks*, Botham and Peter Roebuck, **1986**.

ENGLAND is not ruined because sinewy brown men from a distant colony sometimes hit a ball further and oftener than we do.

J. B. PRIESTLEY.

WHAT will dear mother say when she sees I have travelled 1134 miles to be bowled out first ball?

CHARLES WRIGHT, Lord Hawke's XI *v* Chicago, **1896**.

NAY, I make nowt of it. I'd rather be at Lascelles Hall where I was reared.

EPHRAIM LOCKWOOD, on tour with Daft's team, at Niagara Falls.

AT Peshawar I stayed with a cousin of Jardine. On the first morning we parted on the doorstep, I to play cricket, he to settle a tribal war.

LIONEL LORD, TENNYSON, describing **1937/8** tour of India.

IT's 8.30 on a Friday night; what am I doing in Ahmedabad?

GRAEME FOWLER, England's tour of India **1984**, in Vic Marks' *Marks out of Eleven*, **1985**.

I have from the very outset regarded these tours primarily as imperial enterprises, tending to cement friendship between the Mother Country and her Dominions. Players . . . should not be chosen for their cricket qualities alone. They must be men of good character, high principle, easy of address, and in every personal sense worthy of representing their country in all circumstances, irrespective of their work on the field.

SIR FREDERICK TOONE, three-time manager of Australia, in *Wisden*, **1930**.

WE were fascinated by the milling mass of humanity below and we took to dropping rupees to them and watching them scramble. Unkind, I guess, but it was irresistible. We went a step further and started pouring water on to them as they fought each other for the rupees. We'd fill all available receptacles in the hotel room with water, drop the coins and whoosh.

ALLAN BORDER, Australia's captain, in autobiography of same name, on hotel life in Kanpur, India, **1986**.

NOT everyone . . . is gifted with the temperament and also, may I add, stomach of Albert Trott, to whom everything came alike, fair weather and foul, good food or no food, sleep or no sleep; it was all the same to him – an ideal professor for a tour.

FRANK MITCHELL.

DID I find Test tours too strenuous? The very question is sacrilegious.

ARTHUR MAILEY.

IT was far beyond my imagination . . . that one day a manservant would collect six sets of my flannels and bring them back fastidiously laundered next morning. Every time this happened my mind went back to a leaking tub in a Waterloo backyard, and this one thought seemed to be a basis for every other set of comparative circumstances in my Test career.

ARTHUR MAILEY.

You fellows should never have played cricket if you hate it so much! If I were Sid Smith [the Australian manager] I'd bundle you moaning cows off home straight away.

EDGAR MAYNE, to his discontented team-mates at the Oval during the 1921 Australian tour (quoted by Arthur Mailey).

I persuaded them that to take a towel out to Viv Richards or to dry Clive Lloyd's socks is as good as scoring 20 or 30.

SENATOR WES HALL, West Indies manager, on how he kept the young players happy when not playing on tour of Australia, 1984/5.

THREE to six months of constant packing and unpacking, living out of suitcases with home a succession of impersonal hotel rooms, some good, some bad, the majority indifferent. The tourist's life is in the open, with every move made under the spotlight of publicity. The television lens watches everything on the field, the curious eyes of strangers watch in hotels and streets, at receptions, cocktail parties and a succession of dinners. The moments of complete freedom are few and far between.

JOHN SNOW, Cricket Rebel, 1976.

I don't go along with the argument that the players are under too much pressure and spending too much time away from home. They want to make big money out of the game – well the only way to do so is to tour and play. Players cannot expect to sit on their backsides and be paid for just being Test cricketers. They must work at their profession if that is the profession they want.

BOBBY SIMPSON, former Australian captain, in Howzat, 1980.

LORD Hawke, had he been asked about it, might have taken the same view as I do about having families on tour. It is no more the place for them than a trench on the Somme.

JOHN WOODCOCK, The Times, MCC tour of Australia, 1975.

OUR hotels were turned into kindergartens.

BOB TAYLOR in Standing Up, Standing Back, on presence of wives and children on England's Australian tour, 1974/5.

Wives and families must never tour again with players . . . there is little team spirit and even less fight. Women and children come first for those players who have families. To hell with the pride of England seems to be their motto.

KEITH MILLER, former Australian all-rounder, in *Daily Express*, **1975**.

The gradual exclusion of white folk is a bad thing for the future of West Indies cricket.

LEN HUTTON, first professional to lead England overseas, in the West Indies, **1953/54**.

What this pitch wants is ten minutes of the heavy roller.

JOHN WISDEN on Atlantic, **1859**.
TOM EMMETT on Bay of Biscay, **1876**.

October 6: Beautiful morning, sea smooth. Sports tournament commenced. I got beaten in the first round of peg quoits by Fielder. Had very good deck cricket after tea. Wrote letters and sent postcards. Went to concert in second-class saloon. Passed the Isle of Crete. Saw partial eclipse of the moon. Rather damp atmosphere at night. Dancing on first-class deck. Ship's run: 363 miles.

ALBERT RELF, professional all-rounder, excerpt from diary of MCC's first tour of Australia, **1903/4**.

The match in Rosario was spoilt by the weather . . . but that did not alter the fact that P. F. Warner was only able to field 9 men, which was a great disappointment to Rosario as well as to the Argentine Cricket Association.

E. W. S. THOMSON on Warner's MCC tour of South America, **1927**.

Other points of interest during the passage were the erection of a cricket-net where Bettington alone, owing to the senile lowness of his deliveries, was able to bowl without barking his knuckles on the deck above.

R. C. ROBERTSON-GLASGOW, Cryptics' tour of Gibraltar, **1927**.

NEW Year's Eve was spent somewhere over Uruguay on a DC6, conducted in seasonal community singing by a Roman Catholic priest who used a champagne glass for a baton.

D. R. W. SILK on the MCC tour of Brazil and Argentina, **1958/9**.

Two of the team slept in their cars with windows tightly shut as they heard that mambas could jump, while the remainder removed what they could of the layers of light brown dust from the day's journey and dozed fitfully in the lounge.

ROMANY's tour of South Africa, **1960/61**, the first by a club side as reported in *The Cricketer*.

WHY are we going to this confounded place? Most likely when we get there they [the Boers] will fire at us on the cricket field.

UNNAMED MEMBER (probably Charles Wright) of Lord Hawke's touring team in South Africa on forthcoming visit to Johannesburg in the aftermath of the Jameson Raid.

WE got invitations to coon dances, and on the card 'T.W.B.F.'. On asking what it meant we were informed 'there would be fun' – and there was.

SAMMY WOODS on Arthur Priestley's tour to West Indies, **1897**.

ABOUT four o'clock in the afternoon the engine became 'pumped' and a long halt was made while the machinery was overhauled. The natives, who were (physically) rather a poor looking lot, collected round the team, and a sort of indaba was held by Lord Hawke outside the saloon. This was a splendid chance for the photographers of the team, and one fine nigger, for the magnificent sum of a 'tickey' (3d), formed the centre-piece of a group which included most of the professionals.

PELHAM WARNER in *Cricket Has Many Climes*, describing Lord Hawke's tour of South Africa, **1908**, going up country by train to Bulawayo.

AFTER they were out, Waddy and certain others decided to make a tour of the large Roman Catholic cemetery which adjoined the field. They were scaling a wall, when a policeman sprang up and levelled a firearm at Waddy's head. However, conversation and a judicious use of the ever-ready port bottle saved the situation.

CRYPTICS' tour in Portugal, *The Cricketer*, **1925**.

I made them [cocktails] for the team before breakfast. I don't know what ingredients I mixed with them, still I remember we had to borrow two substitutes at 12 o'clock when we started to play.

SAMMY WOODS on Arthur Priestley's tour to the West Indies, **1897**.

CHRISTMAS Day was a very happy open-air affair – wonderful cold turkey, asparagus, salads and the appropriate liquid accompaniments on the lawn followed by tennis, swimming and other forms of exercise.

ROMANY'S tour of South Africa, **1960/1**.

YOU can't muck around with eggs and you can't muck around with chips.

KEN BARRINGTON explaining his eating habits in India. Quoted in Frank Keating's *Another Bloody Day in Paradise*, **1981**.

THE Church and the Navy were both represented at dinner in our hotel that night; but the navy alone (Lieutenant Allison) accompanied us to a somewhat Neronian evening at the R. A. Mess where, if my memory serves me aright, at least one billiard ball passed out of a closed window.

R. C. ROBERTSON–GLASGOW, Cryptics' tour of Gibraltar, **1927**.

THE formation of a players' committee to deal with the social engagements of the team will, I hope, prevent a repetition of some unfortunate 'incidents' last year, when invitations, accepted for the players, were either totally ignored or treated in a 'casual Australian' manner that must have been intensely irritating to their hosts.

CLEM HILL, former Australian captain, in *The Cricketer*, **1927**.

WE tarried long after the sun had set . . . at . . . Manheim, Philadelphia, where after a bath in a scented swimming pool, we dressed and met beautiful women with whom we danced in the club ballroom or sipped champagne on the terraces.

ARTHUR MAILEY.

CRICKET in Philadelphia took me to far greater imaginative heights than nine Test wickets in Melbourne or 'ten for 66' against Gloucester in 1921.

ARTHUR MAILEY.

AT Rio we stayed a night at Capacabana [sic] Hotel, where we danced on a glass floor, won money at the Casino, and bathed in a glittering sea.

PELHAM WARNER on the MCC tour of South America, **1926/7**.

IT rained from Tuesday to Thursday and cricket was out of the question. There was a racket court, however . . . . There was climbing, a whole day of it, over the Rock in a steady downpour led by an undaunted Sergeant. There was golf at Campo Mento, on the strip of land that joins Gibraltar to Spain, in the course of which Bettington menaced a diminutive caddie with a rather large niblick, for reasons that could only be attributed to liver.

R. C. ROBERTSON-GLASGOW on the expeditions of players on their days off from the Cryptics' tour of Gibraltar, **1927**.

THAT was a good 'un for a trial ball.

CHARLES WRIGHT to bowler after being bowled comprehensively first ball, Lord Hawke's XI *v* Chicago. The ploy did not work.

WELL, Bob, this must be the worst English team ever to reach these shores?

BOB WILLIS's first question on arriving with England team for tour of Australia, **1982**.

NOT bad for the worst team ever to leave England.

MIKE GATTING after the Grand Slam on the same tour.

12

Tribes Without the Law

Pakistanis, Aussies, Yorkies and Others

THE history of Pakistani cricket is one of nepotism, inefficiency, corruption and constant bickering.

IMRAN KHAN, *All Round View*, **1988**.

I am not surprised that the whole of Pakistan is proud of Shakoor. In the history of Pakistan cricket, he will rank along with Hanif, Zaheer, Imran and others for his 'contributions' to Pakistan cricket.

SUNIL GAVASKAR, Indian captain, on umpire Shakoor Rana, **1988**.

PAKISTAN have been cheating us for 37 years and it is getting worse. It was bad enough when I toured in 1951.

TOM GRAVENEY, **1988**.

I was surprised he left one stump standing.

KIM HUGHES, Australia's captain, after Rodney Hogg kicked down stumps in Melbourne Test against Pakistan, **1979**. Hogg had been run out by Javed Miandad while he was inspecting the pitch.

IF we had given them everything they asked for, England would have been out for single figures in each innings and Pakistan would have scored 500 runs in one. They obviously expected a favourable decision on all their appeals, but when 99 per cent are ridiculous and are turned down, the atmosphere becomes edgy and life becomes difficult, if not impossible, for umpires.

KEN PALMER after umpiring the First Test at Edgbaston, **1982**.

AT one stage I was out on the boundary with captain Mike Gatting trying to count the number of Pakistani players on the field. But I gave up because I don't carry a calculator.

MICKY STEWART, England manager, accusing Pakistan of time-wasting by constant substitutions during the First Test at Old Trafford in **1987**.

IF you get one or two bonus decisions then it can make up for some bad luck which goes against you.

HASIB AHSAN, Pakistan manager, on tour in England, **1987**, following wicket-keeper Saleem Yousuf's blatant attempt to cheat out Ian Botham during the Headingley Test.

IF Saleem Yousuf picks up a half-volley, all right, it is called cheating. But everyone is doing it. It has now become absolutely necessary in professional cricket today. Every team is working out strategies in the dressing room on how to pressurise the umpire.

HASIB AHSAN, as above.

THE weather was far from pleasant, so were the opposition, so were the media.

CONFIDENTIAL REPORT by England selectors to the TCCB after the Pakistan tour of England, **1987**.

THE whole thing was just a fly in the ointment.

HASIB AHSAN on the Gatting–Javed altercation in the World Cup.

I will not be making any comment about the pitch or the umpiring, and I want that to be known.

MIKE GATTING, England captain, after England were all out for 175 in the first innings of the Test v Pakistan in Lahore, **1987**.

WE want players to continue to tour here and enjoy their cricket, whoever wins, but if they feel they are competing on unequal terms they won't want to come again and the game will suffer.

PETER LUSH, tour manager, announcing that Broad had been let off with a token reprimand for dissent in the controversial Test v Pakistan in Lahore, **1987**.

WE knew things would happen out here, but we didn't think it would be so blatant. I wouldn't be very happy to win like that. A lot of the decisions against us left a lot to be desired.

MIKE GATTING after England's defeat in the First Test at Lahore, **1987**.

MIKE Gatting used some filthy language to the umpire, and let me tell you, some of the less filthy words are 'bastard' and 'son of a bitch' and so on. No one has a right to abuse umpires.

GENERAL SAFDAR BUTT, President of the Pakistan Cricket Board, after the row between Gatting and Shakoor Rana in the Test at Faisalabad.

I think he is not the son of man. That is why his face is from a white monkey.

LAHORE RAILWAYS DEPOT CHIEF, in letter to Shakoor Rana about Mike Gatting after Faisalabad dispute, **1988**.

I can tell thee, Reagan meeting Gorbachev is nowt compared to this.

DICKIE BIRD on the Gatting–Shakoor confrontation.

I will find it very hard to get the motivation to play another match in Pakistan.

MIKE GATTING after being ordered by the TCCB to send a written apology to Shakoor.

I am going to have a nice quiet family Christmas with the phone off the hook.

MIKE GATTING on his return from Pakistan in **1987**.

BOTH team manager Micky Stewart and Mike Gatting have given us assurances this week that dissent will not occur again. Players cannot behave as they did in Pakistan even if the provocation was immense.

RAMAN SUBBA ROW before the England tour to New Zealand, **1988**.

THE Pakistan tour is finished and we want it dead and buried.

PETER LUSH, England tour manager, arriving in New Zealand in **1988**.

PAKISTAN have been cheating us for 37 years. And by us, I mean other countries as well as England.

MIKE GATTING in Australia two weeks later.

I'D say that perhaps other people hadn't seen the anguish out there. I'd never seen such an unhappy bunch of blokes in my life. In view of the exceptional circumstances of the tour, I thought the payment was warranted.

RAMAN SUBBA ROW, chairman of the TCCB, defending his payment of a £1000 'bad behaviour' bonus to the **1987** England touring team in Pakistan. The TCCB executive committee had subsequently condemned it.

Now we know how Gatting felt.

ANONYMOUS ENGLAND RUGBY PLAYER after England lost 10–9 to France thanks to a disallowed try in **1988**.

WHAT happened between Gatting and me does not seem so ugly after Broad hitting his stumps. Now Dilley has sworn and everybody in the ground has heard his words. Maybe the cricket public will now agree with me that Gatting has bad boys in his team.

SHAKOOR RANA after incidents involving Broad and Dilley in Australia and New Zealand, **1988**.

I'D like to think we'll accept decisions, but I won't be surprised if the umpires go out of their way to be seen to be unbiased. I wouldn't have thought they liked the publicity over the Gatting affair, and I've got a feeling Australia will feel a positive backlash.

ALLAN BORDER, Australian captain, before his team's tour of Pakistan, **1988**.

WHAT are you going to do if you feel you don't have a chance? It is a conspiracy from the word go. The team will do some rethinking and decide about the future of the tour. If the management insist on completing the tour then we will play under protest.

ALLAN BORDER on Pakistani umpiring after Australia lost the First Test in Karachi by an innings and 188 runs, **1988**.

WE were never going to be allowed to win by fair means. The team have voted in favour of stopping the tour right now.

ALLAN BORDER. The tour continued.

WE did not get one leg before decision. Pakistan got six. It seems strange.

BOBBY SIMPSON, the Australian manager, after Australia's defeat in Karachi, **1988**.

WE have outclassed the Australians. It would be cruel to suggest that victory was due to any reason other than our good performances.

INTIKHAB ALAM, Pakistan manager, rejecting Australian protests about the umpiring, Karachi, **1988**.

ALL you Aussies are a bunch of hicks who don't know the first thing about cricket.

IAN BOTHAM's farewell to Australia after Queensland decided not to renew his contract over bad behaviour, **1988**.

I know plenty of professionals whom I would delight to have as guests in my own home, but I am afraid I cannot say the same thing about most of the Australians I have met.

A. W. CARR (Nottinghamshire, England) in *Cricket with the Lid Off*, **1935**.

I have on occasions taken a quite reasonable dislike to the Australians.

TED DEXTER, **1972**.

IN all this Australian team there are barely one or two who would be accepted as public school men.

C. B. FRY, then a journalist, on the **1938** Australians.

THE only time an Australian walks is when his car runs out of petrol.

BARRY RICHARDS, **1980**.

To take the most charitable view of the position, the behaviour of Australian crowds at its best, when judged by the standards accepted in the rest of the world, is not naturally good.

D. R. JARDINE after the Bodyline tour.

I never dreamed that an English crowd would find comedy in Australian batting.

ARTHUR MAILEY on the Old Trafford crowd's response to Mackay's shot against Laker, **1956**.

WHEN you come back from Australia, you feel you've been in Vietnam.

GLENN TURNER, New Zealand batsman, **1983**.

THE air is thick with bad language, the cheating is on a massive scale and the threatening gestures are rife.

BOB TAYLOR in *Standing up, Standing Back*, on attitudes in Sydney schools cricket, **1985**.

I don't think very much of their play but they're a wonderful lot of drinking men.

ROGER IDDISON, member of England's first tour to Australia, on the Australian characteristics, **1861/2**.

WHAT is the world going to think? That Australia has become a namby-pamby nation which doesn't know how to drink? For God's sake, in my day 58 beers between Sydney and London would virtually have classified you as a teetotaller.

IAN CHAPPELL, former Australian Captain, on revelations that batsman David Boon had consumed 58 beers on the team flight to England, 1989. Boon said he was afraid of flying.

IF the Australians did not make cricket their profession in their native land, they most decidedly did when they came to this country; for all who had anything to do with them soon found out how keen they were about '£ s d'.

LILLYWHITE'S CRICKETER'S COMPANION on Australian 'amateurs', 1880.

THE visits of the two Australian XIs to England may be held responsible for the sudden and extraordinary change which took place in the bearing of professionals who had previously comported themselves most becomingly.

LILLYWHITE'S CRICKETERS' COMPANION, 1882.

I always carried powdered resin in my pocket and when the umpire wasn't looking lifted the seam for Jack Gregory and Ted McDonald.

ARTHUR MAILEY, 10 for 66 and All That.

STAY in the slips. You've got a better chance of lifting the seams for Jack [Gregory] and Stork [Hendry] there.

HERBY COLLINS to Arthur Mailey when the latter asked to move to the covers after dropping a catch.

I once saw a bowler in Australia thunder to the wicket and bowl a flat-out underarm to the batsman. No warning given. Quite right, too. In my profession you have to mystify the enemy.

FIELD-MARSHAL VISCOUNT MONTGOMERY.

WE sat in the Windsor Hotel until two in the morning evolving attacking schemes, drawing field placings, thinking of all manner of distractions such as loose bowling sleeves à la Ramadhin, bowlers wearing red caps designed like cricket balls; and even our captain Collins, a man with a rich appreciation of the manly old game, lowered his ideals to such a state that he suggested in all seriousness an ordinary, under-arm 'grubber'.

ARTHUR MAILEY on the Australian team's desperation after Hobbs and Sutcliffe had batted all day in **1924/5**. The next day Mailey bowled Hobbs first ball with a full toss!

IT was an act of cowardice and I consider it appropriate that the Australians were wearing yellow.

ROBERT MULDOON, New Zealand Prime Minister, on Trevor Chappell's underarm delivery with 6 needed to win off the final ball, Melbourne, **1981**.

FAIR dinkum, Greg, how much pride do you sacrifice to win 35,000 dollars?

IAN CHAPPELL, **1981** (his brother Greg was captain).

ROD MARSH: Plan A is to fight fire with fire . . . in other words, try to crack a few skulls.
GREG CHAPPELL: No, Rod, it's beers that are for cracking; heads are for using thoughtfully.

THE AUSTRALIAN WICKET-KEEPER'S plan to beat the West Indies is rejected by his captain, **1984**.

WE don't play this game for fun.

WILFRED RHODES, Yorkshire spin bowler.

CRICKET was never made for any championship. . . . Cricket's a game, not a competition.

GEORGE HIRST, Yorkshire all-rounder.

SOMEONE born within the sound of Bill Bowes.

MIKE CAREY, *Daily Telegraph*, definition of a Yorkshireman.

DON'T tell me his average or his top score at Trent Bridge. How many runs, how many wickets did he get against Yorkshire?

D. R. JARDINE'S standard for judging potential Test cricketers.

THE trouble with you damn Yorkshiremen is that you are only interested in playing this game to win.

FORMER ENGLAND CAPTAIN to Fred Trueman during tour of Australia.

IT is the bugbear of Yorkshiremen that they always feel that they have to behave like Yorkshiremen, or like their fixed belief in what a Yorkshireman should be: tough, ruthless, brave, mean.

ALAN GIBSON in *The Cricketer*, **1978**.

GERRUP, tha's makin' an exhibition o' thiself.

ARTHUR 'TICKER' MITCHELL to Yorkshire colleague Ellis Robinson after spectacular diving catch.

THERE were telegrams from all over the place – except Yorkshire, of course.

FRED TRUEMAN, recalling his feat of becoming the first man to take 300 Test wickets, England *v* Australia at the Oval, **1964**. (From *The Ashes: Highlights since 1948*, 1989.)

IT would scarcely be human not to be amused by the flounders of Yorkshire County Cricket in search of a captain.

GUARDIAN LEADER, **1927**. (Herbert Sutcliffe had declined the opportunity to become Yorkshire's first professional captain.)

WHAT'S tha think it is – t'bloody Scarborough Festival?

PARK AVENUE SPECTATOR to John Hampshire, after rapid 42 for Yorkshire *v* Australians, **1964**.

ONE of Yorkshire's faults is that some of the older players live in the past and give the impression that things are no longer good. Some younger players can't stand talking to them. The game is as good as ever. It's just played under different conditions.

JOHNNY WARDLE, ex-Yorkshire and England left-arm spin bowler, during tragically brief return to county as assistant bowling coach, **1985**.

WE'VE no great stars but we've got 11 or 12 bloody good cricketers.

PHIL CARRICK, **1987**.

ANY injury at all to key players proves that with our 'Yorkshire-born' policy we do not compete on equal terms and always have our backs to the wall.

A DISILLUSIONED CARRICK, calling for the Yorkshire-only restriction to be scrapped, two years later.

THE Yorkshire stable: worth a flutter in the championship?

CAPTION in *The Cricketer*, pre-season preview, **1989**.

I never thought it would come to this. Just think – waiting for a result at Pontypridd.

YORKSHIRE COMMITTEE MAN. Yorkshire would have finished bottom of the championship in **1989** if Glamorgan had taken seven points from their last match against Worcestershire at Pontypridd. They didn't.

WE shake hands on t'first morning and say: 'How do?'; then we say nowt for three days, but: 'How's that?'

ROY KILNER on **1920s** Lancashire *v* Yorkshire matches. Also ascribed to Emmott Robinson.

THEY play the most miserable game and set the most miserable example for the whole country of how games should be played.

DR CYRIL NORWOOD, Headmaster of Harrow School, on Roses matches, **1929**.

I think people are rather tired of seeing a certain county playing in Eastbourne. We sent a protest to the county and were told that we were too late, so we are to have them again this year.

ALDERMAN KAY, at traditional Mayor's Luncheon during Eastbourne Festival week, **1931**. The offending county, which shunned the luncheon, was Lancashire.

THERE'S no question that being a New Zealander was a bad start in a cricketing sense. We all lacked confidence at birth I guess. We could see the tough way Australians played and longed to be able to do that, to give them a battle. We were the nice guys.

RICHARD HADLEE in *At the Double*, **1985**.

I'VE been surprised at the insolence and the high and mighty attitude of some of the younger Kiwis.

GREG CHAPPELL, **1981**.

YOU wait until New Zealand tour West Indies in 1982. We will get our own back with our umpires.

DERYCK MURRAY, West Indian wicket-keeper, after the controversial Test series in New Zealand, **1980**.

IF the West Indies are on top, they're magnificent. If they are down, they grovel. And with the help of Brian Close and a few others, I intend to make them grovel.

TONY GREIG, England captain, before the 1976 series. The West Indies won the series 3–0.

I recommend that future tours to the West Indies should take a good umpire to teach them various laws of the game, of which at the moment the majority are a bit doubtful.

HON. F. S. G. CALTHORPE, MCC captain, tour of West Indies, **1926**.

THERE'S no way at all we should lose. If we do, then a few heads will roll. You could bat for ten days on this pitch and not get a result.

IAN BOTHAM, England's captain, during First Test against West Indies, **1981** (they lost).

WHEN I said that heads would roll, I obviously didn't mean I'd be out there chopping off heads. The media have taken it out of context.

IAN BOTHAM after England lost the Test by an innings.

EVEN when they are just spectators, there is something intimidating about their presence.

SIR LEN HUTTON on West Indian cricketers, **1981**.

IT is the constant, vigilant, bold and shameless manipulation of players to exclude black players that had so demoralised West Indian teams and exasperated the people.

C. L. R. JAMES, *Beyond a Boundary*, **1963**.

THE members were elegant youths of the Pradhu caste and promised very well at first, but their kilted garments interfered with running and they threw the ball when fielding in the same fashion as boarding-school girls. They talked beautiful English, and were perfectly up in English slang, but I was sorry to see their ardour cool.

REPORT on the formation of the Bombay Union CC, the first Hindu club, in **1866**. (Cited by F. S. Ashley-Cooper in *The Cricketer*, **1927**, no source given.)

YOU could feel each delivery double declutch on pitching.

COLIN COWDREY on the slow Indian wickets, **1963/4**.

MOST responsible Indian officials would admit that the assurance of five full days' gate money was equally important to them as an interesting finish.

COLIN COWDREY.

IMPORT restriction is so severe that their leading players cannot obtain top quality equipment and if we have achieved nothing else, at least we have furnished their Test players with adequate bats, pads, gloves and boots.

COLIN COWDREY.

IT is in the matter of patience that I think the Indian will never be equal to the Englishman.

LORD HARRIS, *A Few Short Runs*. **1921**.

A well-captained Parsi, Mohammedan and Hindu side would do better than a mixed one . . . but few Anglo-Indian cricketers could hold out strong hopes of such a side being well-captained.

E. H. D. SEWELL.

PAKISTAN is the sort of place every man should send his mother-in-law to, for a month, all expenses paid.

IAN BOTHAM on returning from the **1984** tour.

IF cricket is regarded, even unconsciously, as an imported game, a freak amusement of an alien race, its roots are shallow.

SIR HILARY BLOOD, on slow progress of cricket in Ceylon, **1955**.

WHAT was once to him an insipid form of recreation is now a new religion and such is his temperament and personality that in years to come he will be an even more faithful patron than his less volatile English counterpart.

PETER POLLOCK, South African quickie, on Afrikaaners' growing affection for cricket, **1967**.

I would not have it. They would have expected him to throw boomerangs during the luncheon interval.

CECIL RHODES, explaining why he did not include a coloured player on the South African tour of England which he financed, **1894/5**.

To people who kick footballs barefoot and who tread ceremonially on white-hot stones, the impact of a small leather ball at speed is no noteworthy affair.

PHILIP SNOW, founder of Fiji Cricket Association, BBC Radio, **1951**.

WHERE the English language is unspoken there can be no real cricket.

NEVILLE CARDUS.

IF the French noblesse had been capable of playing cricket with their peasants, their châteaux would never have been burnt.

G. M. TREVELYAN, *English Social History*, **1944**.

THIS picturesque view is, to my mind, open to question. It is surely more probable that the combination of Latin temperament and bodyline bowling would have accelerated it [the Revolution].

IAN PEEBLES.

PARIS, 16 APRIL: on Monday last, a cricket match was played by some English Gentlemen in the Champ Elyses [sic]. His Grace of Dorset was, as usual, the most distinguished for skill and activity. The French, however, cannot imitate us in such vigorous exertions of the body; so that they rarely enter the lists.

THE TIMES, **1786**.

CRICKET is the pride and the privilege of the Englishman alone. Into this, his noble and favourite amusement, no other people ever pretended to penetrate: a Frenchman or a German would not know which end of the bat they were to hold; and so fine, so scientific and so elaborate is the skill regarding it, that only a small part of England have as yet acquired a knowledge of it.

REV. JOHN MITFORD, *Gentleman's Magazine*, **1833**.

RANGOON cricketers as a class may be termed stay-at-home, so few and far between are visits to or from Burma's neighbours.

'CRICKET IN BURMA'. *The Cricketer*, **1928**.

THE players wear little more than is demanded by the laws of decency, the torrid climate making clothes superfluous, while the pitch is framed in palm-trees.

GEORGE CECIL, 'Cricket in Papua', *The Cricketer*, **1928**.

WICKET-KEEPING has always been a particularly bright feature of American cricket.

G. L. JESSOP.

MEN, women, boys and girls form the respective elevens. The players' bodies are lavishly smeared with coconut oil, flowers are stuck in the hair, the young girls (some of whom are well favoured) sport tinkling shell earrings, necklaces and bangles. All laugh at hits and misses.

GEORGE CECIL.

IT is really remarkable how well the Danes play. Undoubtedly they have the right temperament for the game – denied to the Latin races.

REPORT in *The Cricketer* on the Incogniti tour of Denmark, **1927**.

PERSONALLY I have no wish to re-create in a corner of a foreign field the 'English' game with ten other pining expatriates. I live and work in Italy and want to play cricket in an Italian League and alongside Italian players as well as other expatriates.

J. P. LEECH, Pianoro-Bologna de Paz CC, on the ruling by the Italian Cricket Association limiting the number of non-Italian players to four in each team, which disqualified the expatriate Milan and Euratom clubs from competition, **1988**.

IN Italy we don't have good net facilities.

ALFONSO JAJERAYAH, captain of the **1985** Italian touring side.

WEST Indians, that's what we could do with.

JERRY WELLS, a member of the Italian touring team, **1988**.

ON the Himalayas I have fielded and bowled wearing a mackintosh.

E. H. D. SEWELL on his cricketing days in India in the **1890s**.

13
Ladies in Waiting

Players, Wives, Supporters and Others

I was fascinated by an adorable girl.

TED DEXTER, explaining his delayed arrival for his first season at Sussex following Cambridge University's tour of Copenhagen, **1957**.

I'M very sorry, my Lord, but I've been lunching with a lady.

C. J. M. FOX apologising to Lord Harris for a late return from lunch against Kent.

WE'VE always set the trend. Remember, women cricketers were the first to bowl overarm.

RACHEL HEYHOE-FLINT, requesting women's Test at Lord's during the National Association's 50th anniversary, **1975**.

LADIES playing cricket – absurd. Just like a man trying to knit.

ANONYMOUS EX-ENGLAND CAPTAIN (male) to Brian Johnston.

PITCHES are like wives; you can never tell how they're going to turn out.

LEN HUTTON, explaining why he put Australia in to bat at Brisbane, MCC tour, **1954/5**.

LAST week, at Sileby feast, the women so far forgot themselves as to enter a game of cricket, and by their deportment as well as frequent applications to the tankard, they rendered themselves objects such as no husband, parent or lover could contemplate with any degree of satisfaction.

NOTTINGHAM REVIEW, **1833**.

THEY moved very slowly from one side of the ground to the other. They also complained about the sun's reflection off parked cars. We are just not used to these sort of tactics.

AUDREY COLLINS, Women's Cricket Association, after India had bowled only eight overs in the penultimate hour of the England v India match at Collingham, near Leeds, 1986.

PROFESSIONAL coaching is a man trying to get you to keep your legs close together when other men had spent a lifetime trying to get them wider apart.

RACHEL HEYHOE-FLINT, former England women's captain.

SOME women think that because they play a masculine game they have to look masculine. Some women associated with women's cricket are only ever seen in chunky sweaters and slacks. I get to the stage where I feel embarrassed with some of them.

RACHEL HEYHOE-FLINT.

I'VE urged cameramen to seek out a bronzed Aussie male but there doesn't appear to be too many of them, especially among those who drink 15 tinnies a day.

TONY GREIG, defending Channel 9's cutaway shots of scantily clad female spectators, 1987.

I wish you'd speak to Mary, Nurse,
She's really getting worse and worse.
Just now when Tommy gave her out
She cried and then began to pout.
And then she tried to take the ball
Although she cannot bowl at all.
And now she's standing on the pitch,
The miserable little Bitch!

HILAIRE BELLOC, The Game of Cricket.

'I think it's simply sickening the way girls want to do everything we do,' said Norris disgustedly.

'Well, she's only thirteen. Seems to me a jolly healthy symptom. Laudable ambition and that sort of thing.' Well, I sent some down. She played 'em like a book. Bit inclined to pull, all girls are. So I put in a long hop to the off and she let go at it like Jessop. Smashed my second finger into hash.

P. G. WODEHOUSE, *A Prefect's Uncle*.

BATES is a fool! 'E's gone and got married id middle o'soomer. 'E should have got married id middle o'winter so that 'e could pay 'is undivided attention to it.

TED PEATE, Yorkshire spinner, on team-mate Billy Bates.

AT Tunstall she came to the ground with me every morning and afternoon. I asked her to come there to bat at the nets so that I could practise my spin bowling. Day after day for two solid seasons she helped me in this way, and many's the time she's gone home with her finger nails turned black and blue by blows from my bowling. Scores of times I have seen her crying with pain through these blows as she stood there patiently holding the bat and trying to defend her wicket against my 'spinners'; but she never gave up.

CECIL PARKIN, on his wife.

WE had cricket for breakfast, dinner and tea. It was like an obsession bordering on madness. He could tell you who scored what years ago – and even what the weather was like. But he could not remember my birthday unless I reminded him.

MILDRED ROWLEY, divorcing her husband Mike, scorer for Stourbridge CC, **1981**.

REALLY there is nothing more that I can say. I cannot stop . . . we have got to get on with the game.

MIKE ROWLEY, on tour at the time with Worcestershire Marauders, **1981**.

WHEN we were living in Sydney a friend told me that one night, while she and her husband were making love, she suddenly noticed something sticking in his ear. When she asked him what it was he replied, 'Be quiet! I'm listening to the cricket.'

VICKY RANTZEN, the *Observer*, **1978**.

IF possible tour with a bachelor team or a side of 'grass-widowers'.

D. L. A. JEPHSON's advice on club tours.

TEN out of eleven women care very little for cricket for cricket's sake, and though from the goodness of their hearts they insist on coming to the grounds and sitting through the weary hours till at length they grow tired, restless, fretful, it would be kinder to all concerned, and less like cruelty to animals, to leave them quietly at home.

D. L. A. JEPHSON.

THERE are men who fear women more than they love cricket.

GEOFF SCARGILL, Lancashire annual meeting, proposing women should be allowed into Old Trafford pavilion, **1985**.

LET them in and the next thing you know the place will be full of children.

LANCASHIRE MEMBER, opposing resolution.

SURPRISINGLY, we are told that it is the younger members that we are up against.

MAUREEN FITZGIBBON, Lancashire 'lady subscriber' stepping up the campaign for full membership for women. They won the two-thirds majority later in **1989**.

WE are told that the speaker joined the club as Mr K. Hull.

BOB BENNETT, Lancashire chairman, **1989** annual meeting, explaining how the county's first woman member, Stephanie Lloyd had sneaked through the net before a sex-change operation.

THE MCC should change their name to MCP.

DIANA EDULJI, Indian Women's touring team captain, on being refused entry to the Lord's Pavilion during the men's Test, **1986.**

OH, tush, I'm in a state of shock. Five minutes ago my chap was bowled by Freddie Titmus.

MARIE-LISE PIERROT, companion of actor John Hurt, on being ordered out of the Lord's Pavilion, **1988.**

IF a lot of people thought it was a frightfully good idea, we would follow it through, but I feel there is not a hope in hell of that.

LT COL JOHN STEPHENSON, Secretary MCC, on the ballot asking members whether women should be admitted, **1989.**

POPULAR opinion would be wrong if it ever thought that the M in MCC could stand for misogyny. Quite the reverse is the case. But it may well be that in this changing world there would be one small part of a small part of London which affords refuge for the hunted male animal.

JACK BAILEY, former MCC secretary, arguing against admission of women into the Lord's pavilion, **1989.**

MCC have never yet subscribed to the freedom of thought which goes hand in hand with the unisex sauna.

JACK BAILEY.

I was joyous and I did cry and laugh at the same time and I thanked the kind Lord of being so good to an old lady.

MRS MARIE STUART, grandmother of Barbados-born Roland Butcher, on hearing he had been chosen to play cricket for England in tour of West Indies, **1980.**

OH God, if there be cricket in heaven, let there also be rain.

LORD HOME, from *Prayer of a Cricketer's Wife.*

14
Literary Lions

Great Writers on the Great Game

The Judge to dance his brother serjeant call,
The Senator at cricket urge the ball.

ALEXANDER POPE, *The Dunciad*, **1742**. The lines are believed to refer to Lord John Sackville.

England, when once of peace and wealth possessed,
Began to think frugality a jest;
So are polite; hence all her well-bred heirs
Gamesters and Jockeys turned, and Cricket-players.

SOAME JENYNS, political satirist, **1700s**.

When Death (for Lords must die) your doom shall seal,
What sculptured Honors shall your tomb reveal?
Instead of Glory, with a weeping eye,
Instead of Virtue pointing to the sky,
Let Bats and Balls th'affronted stone disgrace,
While Farce stands leering by, with Satyr face,
Holding, with forty notches mark'd, a board –
The noble triumph of a noble Lord!

ANONYMOUS PAMPHLET lampooning the Duke of Dorset, ardent cricketer and Whig politician, **1778**.

SOMETIMES an unlucky boy will drive his cricket ball full in my face.

DR JOHNSON in *The Rambler*, **1750**.

WE were a nest of singing birds. Here we walked, there we played cricket.

DR JOHNSON on his days at Pembroke College, Oxford.

CRICKET. A sport in which contenders drive a ball with sticks in opposition to each other.

DR JOHNSON, *Dictionary of the English Language*, 1755.

Attend all ye Muses, and join to rehearse
An old English Sport, never praised yet in verse.
'Tis Cricket I sing, of illustrious fame,
No nation e'er boasted so noble a game . . .

When we've played our last game and our fate shall draw nigh
(For the heroes of cricket like others must die)
Our Bats we'll resign, neither troubled nor vexed,
And surrender our wickets to those who come next.

REV. REYNELL COTTON, first and last verses of *Hambledon Cricket Song*, 1767.

Yet all in public, and in private, strive
To keep the ball of action still alive,
And, just to all, when each his ground has run,
Death tips the wicket, and the game is done.

JAMES LOVE, *The Game of Cricket* (last 4 lines).

Hail, Cricket! glorious manly, British Game!
First of all Sports! be first alike in Fame!

JAMES LOVE, *Cricket: an Heroic Poem*, opening couplet, 1744.

That Bill's a foolish fellow;
He has given me a black eye.
He does not know how to handle a bat
Any more than a dog or a cat;
He has knock'd down the wicket,
And broke his stumps,
And runs without shoes to save his pumps.

WILLIAM BLAKE, final stanza of *The Song of Tilly Lally*.

When all the nations throng the Judgement hill
Where Peter, with his great keys, guards the wicket,
England, in lazy flannels lounging, will
Question the Fisherman: Did you play cricket?

IRISH VERSE.

CAPITAL game – smart sport – fine exercise – very.

ALFRED JINGLE in Charles Dickens' *Pickwick Papers*, **1836**.

THE scouts were hot and tired; the bowlers were changed and bowled till their arms ached; but Dumkins and Podder remained unconquered. Did an elderly gentleman essay to stop the progress of the ball, it rolled between his legs or slipped between his fingers. Did a slim gentleman try to catch it, it struck him on the nose, and bounded pleasantly off with redoubled violence, while the slim gentleman's eye filled with water, and his form writhed with anguish. Was it thrown straight up to the wicket, Dumkins had reached it before the ball. In short, when Dumkins was caught out and Podder stumped out, All-Muggleton had notched some fifty-four while the score of the Dingley Dellers was as blank as their faces.

AS ABOVE.

FAITHFUL attendant – Quanko Samba – last man left – sun so hot, bat in blisters, ball scorched brown – five hundred and seventy runs – rather exhausted – Quanko mustered up last remaining strength – bowled me out – had a bath, and went out to dinner.

MR JINGLE'S account of a single-wicket match in the West Indies, Charles Dickens, *Pickwick Papers*.

POOR Quanko – never recovered it – bowled on, on my account – bowled off, on his own – died, sir.

AS ABOVE.

'BUT it's more than a game. It's an institution,' said Tom.
'Yes,' said Arthur, 'the birthright of British boys, old and young, as
habeas corpus and trial by jury are of British men.'

THOMAS HUGHES, *Tom Brown's Schooldays*, **1857**.

> If the wild bowler thinks he bowls,
>   Or if the batsman thinks he's bowled,
> They know not, poor misguided souls,
>   They too shall perish unconsoled.
> I am the batsman and the bat,
>   I am the bowler and the ball,
> The umpire, the pavilion cat,
>   The roller, pitch, and stumps, and all.

ANDREW LANG, *Brahma*.

> There's a breathless hush in the Close tonight,
> Ten to make and the last man in,
> And it's not for the sake of a ribboned coat
> Or the selfish hope of a season's fame
> But his Captain's hand on his shoulder smote:
> Play up! Play up! and play the Game!

HENRY NEWBOLT, from *Vitai Lampada*, **1877**.

> Now in Maytime to the wicket
>   Out I march with bat and pad;
> See the son of grief at cricket
>   Trying to be glad.

A. E. HOUSMAN, *A Shropshire Lad*, **1896**.

'CRICKET', said Raffles, 'like everything else is a good enough sport
until you discover a better. . . . What's the satisfaction of taking a
man's wicket when you want his spoons? Still, if you can bowl a bit
your low cunning won't get rusty, and always looking for the weak
spot's just the kind of mental exercise one wants!'

E. W. HORNUNG, *Raffles, the Amateur Cracksman*, **1899**.

Thank God, who made the British Isles
And taught me how to play;
I do not worship crocodiles,
Or bow the knee to clay!
Give me a willow wand and I
With hide and cork and twine,
From century to century
Will gambol round my shrine.

RUDYARD KIPLING, *Cricket Humour*.

Then ye returned to your trinkets;
Then ye contented your souls
With the flanelled fools at the wicket
Or the muddied oafs at the goals.

RUDYARD KIPLING, *The Islanders*, **1902**.

Wake! for the Ruddy Ball has taken flight
That scatters the slow wicket of the Night;
    And the swift batsman of the Dawn has driven
Against the star-spiked Rails a fiery smite.

FRANCIS THOMPSON, *Wake! for the Ruddy Ball has taken flight*.

It is little I repair to the matches of the Southron folk,
Though my own red roses there may blow;
It is little I repair to the matches of the Southron folk,
Though the red roses crest the caps I know.
For the field is full of shades as I near the shadowy coast,
And a ghostly batsman plays to the bowling of a ghost,
And I look through my tears on a soundless-clapping host,
As the run-stealers flicker to and fro, to and fro,
O my Hornby and my Barlow long ago!

FRANCIS THOMPSON, *At Lord's*, **1907**.

'By Hobbs,' cried Archie, as he began to put away the porridge, 'I feel as fit as anything this morning. I'm asbolutely safe for a century.'

'You shouldn't boast with your mouth full,' Myra told her brother.

A. A. MILNE, 'The Rabbits' in *The Day's Play*, **1910**.

WHEN I said we weren't very good, I only meant we didn't make many runs. Mr Simpson is a noted fast bowler, the Major has an MCC scarf, which can be seen quite easily at point, and I keep wicket. Between us we dismiss many a professor. Just as they are shaping for a cut, you know, they catch sight of the Major's scarf, lose their heads, and give me an easy catch.

A. A. MILNE, 'The Rabbits' in *The Day's Play*, **1910**.

. . . Walking he rumbled and grumbled,
    Scolding himself and not me;
    One glove was off, and he fumbled,
    Twisting the other hand free.

ARTHUR CONAN DOYLE, *A Reminiscence of Cricket* (stanza 18 of 'The day he bowled W. G. Grace').

To have been a batsman does not weaken
    The reverence paid to an archdeacon,
    And every bishop knows it biases
    The public favour in his diocese.

ROBERT BRIDGES.

I see them in foul dug-outs, gnawed by rats,
    And in the ruined trenches, lashed by rain,
    Dreaming of things they did with balls and bats.

SIEGFRIED SASSOON, from *The Dreamers*.

OH, I am so glad you have begun to take an interest in cricket. It is simply a social necessity in England.

P. G. WODEHOUSE, *Piccadilly Jim*, **1918**.

AT everything else Chrystal's one of the smartest chaps you ever met, though he does weigh you and me put together, and quite one of the best. But he's so mad keen on cricket that he keeps a pro. for himself and his son of seven, and by practising more than any man in England he scores his ten runs in all matches every season.

E. W. HORNUNG, 'Chrystal's Century' from *Old Offenders and a Few Old Scores*, **1923**.

I set about consulting the omens for my success in the match. I searched assiduously through the first-class scores, picking out the amateurs whose names, like my own, began with 'S', and whose initial was 'G'. There were only two that day: the result was most unsatisfactory. G. Shaw: run out, 1; G. Smith: c. Lilley, b. Field, 0. According to that I should score half a run. So I called in professional assistance, and was rewarded with Shrewsbury; not out, 127.

SIEGFRIED SASSOON, *Memoirs of a Fox-Hunting Man*, **1928**.

WHILE we were walking across the fields Aunt Evelyn paused on the top of a stile to remark that she felt sure Mr Balfour would be a splendid Prime Minister. But I was meditating about Shrewsbury's innings. How I wished I could bat like him, if only for one day!

SIEGFRIED SASSOON, as above.

[PARSON Yalden] enunciated the grace in slightly unparsonic tones, which implied that he was not only Rector of Rotherden but also a full member of MCC and first cousin once removed to Lord Chatwynd.

SIEGFRIED SASSOON, as above.

I well remember . . . at my Big School, after I missed a catch at long-leg, saying to myself 'O Lord, take away my life, for I am not worthy to live!'

JOHN COWPER POWYS, *Autobiography*.

IT is that cricket field that, in all the sharp and bitter moments of life as they come to me now, gives me a sense of wholesome proportion: 'At least I am not playing cricket!'

JOHN COWPER POWYS.

A tower we must have, and a clock in the tower,
Looking over the tombs, the tithe barn, the bower;
The inn and the mill, the forge and the hall,
And that loamy sweet level that loves bat and ball.

And now where the confident cuckoo takes flight
Over buttercups kindled in millions last night,
A labourer leans on the stackyard's low wall
With the hens bothering round him, and dreams bat and ball.

EDMUND BLUNDEN, *The Season Opens* (stanzas 1 and 4).

The sun in the heavens was beaming;
The breeze bore an odour of hay,
My flannels were spotless and gleaming,
My heart was unclouded and gay;
The ladies, all gaily apparelled,
Sit round looking on at the match,
In the tree-tops the dicky-birds carolled,
All was peace till I bungled that catch.

P. G. WODEHOUSE, *Missed!* (first stanza).

I doubt if there is any game in the world more animating or delightful than a cricket match – I do not mean a set match at Lord's ground for money, hard money, between certain gentlemen and players, as they are called – people who make a trade of that noble sport and degrade it into an affair of betting and hedgings and cheatings, it may be like boxing or horse racing . . . NO! The cricket I mean is a real, solid, old-fashioned match between neighbouring parishes where each attacks the other from honour and a supper, glory and half-a-crown a man.

MARY RUSSELL MITFORD, *A Country Cricket Match*, 1932.

DRINKING the best tea in the world on an empty cricket ground – that, I think, is the final pleasure left to man.

C. P. SNOW, *Death Under Sail*, 1932.

THE innings closed at 69, Donald not out nought. Opinion on the gaffers' bench, which corresponded in years and connoisseurship very closely with the Pavilion at Lord's, was sharply divided on the question whether 69 was, or was not, a winning score.

A. G. MACDONNELL, *England, Their England.*

GENERAL BURROUGHS: Do you remember Wilmington?
GENERAL FAVERSHAM: Wilmington?
GENERAL BURROUGHS: Fine old service family. Father killed at Inkermann, grandfather blown up under Nelson, an uncle scalped by Indians – oh, splendid record, splendid.
GENERAL FAVERSHAM: What happened?
GENERAL BURROUGHS: Well the general ordered him to gallop through the front lines with a message. Paralysed with funk. Couldn't move. General sent his adjutant, killed before he'd gone 50 yards. Sent his ADC – head blown off. Then he went through with the message himself, lost his arm. Ruined his cricket.

FROM THE FILM, *The Four Feathers*, **1939**.

CALDICOTT: That German officer looked a lot like old Dickie Randall. You know him, used to bowl slow leg-breaks. He played for the Gentlemen once – caught and bowled for a duck as I remember.
CHARTERS: You think he's a traitor then?
CALDICOTT: But he played for the Gentlemen!
CHARTERS: Ah, but only once.

FROM THE FILM, *Night Train to Munich*, **1940**.

THEY vanish, these immortal players, and we suddenly realize with astonishment that years have passed since we heard a passing mention of some of them. At one point they seem as much a part of the permanent scheme of things as the sun which glows upon their familiar faces and attitudes and the grass which makes the background for their portrait; and then, bless us, it is time even for them to go.

EDMUND BLUNDEN, *Cricket Country*, **1944**.

CRICKET is a game full of forlorn hopes and sudden dramatic changes of fortune, and its rules are so ill-defined that their interpretation is partly an ethical business. It is not a 20th century game and nearly all modern-minded people dislike it.

GEORGE ORWELL, essay, *Raffles and Miss Blandish*, **1944**.

Cricket, lovely cricket,
At Lord's where I saw it;
They gave the crowd plenty fun;
Second Test and West Indies won.
With these two little pals of mine
Ramadhin and Valentine.

LORD BEGINNER, *Victory Calypso*, **1950**.

IT wasn't cricket; it wasn't cricket that an elderly gnome-like individual with a stringy neck and creaking joints should, by dint of head-work and superior cunning, reverse the proverb that youth will be served. It was an ascendancy of brain over brawn, of which, like a true Englishman, I felt suspicious.

L. P. HARTLEY, *The Go-Between*, **1953**.

IT was a very different half-century from Mr Maudsley's, a triumph of luck, not cunning, for the will, and even the wish to win seemed absent from it. Dimly I felt that the contrast represented something more than the conflict between hall and village. It was that, but it was also the struggle between order and lawlessness, between obedience to tradition and defiance of it, between social stability and revolution, between one attitude to life and another.

L. P. HARTLEY, as above.

SAM: You shouldn't have done that, skipper . . . standing back like that. It was you they wanted to applaud, not me.
JARVIS (*ironically*): You think that's the way it sounded, Sam?
SAM (*gruffly*): Sorry about getting out, anyway.
JARVIS: It doesn't matter, Sam. There's plenty on the board and they can't beat us now.
SAM (*muttering*): All the same, I'd have liked to have given them something to cheer about.
JARVIS: You have, Sam.

EXCERPT from *The Final Test*, film starring Jack Warner as Sam Palmer, out for a duck in the Oval Test, **1953**.

WAIT a moment, wait a moment. The most extraordinary thing is happening. The whole Australian team is waiting by the wicket and Jarvis is standing back to let Palmer walk into the pavilion alone. And listen to the applause. Listen. (*There is the sound of growing applause, mingled with cheers and shouts of 'Good Old Sam'.*)
(*Voice in a frenzy of excitement*) . . . and they're getting up all round the ground. All round the ground they're standing. This for a man who was out fourth ball. The whole ground – thirty thousand people – standing and cheering – the Australians cheering too – cheering the man they've just dismissed for a duck.

COMMENTATOR in the film *The Final Test*, on Sam Palmer's dismissal, **1953**.

> He leaps once more, with eager spring,
> To catch the brief-glimpsed flying ball
> And quickens to its sudden sting:
> The brightness dies: the old eyes fall,
> They see, but do not understand,
> A pursed, rheumatic, useless hand.

JOHN ARLOTT, from *The Old Cricketer*.

> Though wayward Time be changeful as Man's Will
> We have the game, we have the Oval still,
> And still the Gas-Works mark the Gas-Works End
> And still our sun shines and the rain descends.

JOHN MASEFIELD, opening verse of 'Eighty-Five to Win', celebrating England *v* Australia, The Oval **1882**, from *The Bluebell and Other Verses*, 1961.

AT Baron's Lodge there was no suggestion, as there was at so many schools, that skill at cricket implied moral excellence or that the game itself was a proving ground for life.

SIMON RAVEN, *Close of Play*, **1964**.

JENNY was pleased for Graham, who looked very dangerous in his wicket-keeper's pads and gloves. She had known he would be as good at stumping as trying could make you. He was much freer in his movements on the field than he ever was off it, making great jumps at balls he had no hope of reaching, clapping his gloves together to encourage fielders to throw to him, leaving his arms up in the air for a quarter of a minute when once he missed a ball and it went to the boundary behind him.

KINGSLEY AMIS, *Take a Girl Like You*, **1960**.

FOR my own sake too I wished that time might stop; that I might stand for ever in the sun, while the trees rustled and the young voices laughed along the terrace, and watch my darling so beautiful and happy at his play. But time slipped on, and my darling started to sweat like a cart-horse, and the Scholars were faced with shameful defeat.

SIMON RAVEN, *Fielding Gray*, **1969**.

As in life so in death lies a bat of renown
Slain by a lorry (three ton);
His innings is over, his bat is laid down;
To the end a poor judge of a run.

GEORGE MCWILLIAM, Epitaph.

MOON: Sometimes I dream of revolution, a bloody coup d'Etat by the second rank – troupes of actors slaughtered by their under-studies, magicians sawn in half by indefatigably smiling glamour girls, cricket teams wiped out by marauding bands of twelfth men.

TOM STOPPARD, *The Real Inspector Hound*, **1968**.

MIRIAM: I don't know if I prefer Rog to have a good innings or a bad one: If it's a good one, he relives it in bed, shot by shot, and if it's a bad one he actually replays the shots until he gets it right. He can make a really good innings last all winter.

RICHARD HARRIS, *Outside Edge*.

OTHER early arrivals left deep footprints in the dew; Charlie Fox, who was running the beer tent, appeared, rolling a barrel like a carpet across the grass. The cricketers were jealously fencing off their stretch of green wicket so that no-one would set foot on the sacred twenty-two yards, while other players set up the beat-the-batsman sideshow.

LESLIE THOMAS, *The Dearest and the Best*, **1984**.

TOMMY JUDD: You know what I really hate about cricket – it's such a damn good game.
GUY BENNETT: Ah, Judd's paradox . . . of course, cricket is a fundamental part of the capitalist conspiracy. One only has to observe the sylvan scene – there's the proletariat forced to labour in the field while the bourgeoisie indulges in the pleasures of batting and bowling.
JUDD: Hmm, quite.
BENNETT: I mean, there's every reason to suppose that the game ultimately derives from the wholly unjustified right of the medieval lord to the unpaid labour of villeins and serfs at haymaking and harvest.
JUDD: You know, you're really beginning to get the idea.
BENNETT: Thanks.

JULIAN MITCHELL, *Another Country*, **1984**. (Judd a communist student, and Bennett, a homosexual, are watching a cricket match at Eton.)

While batting once, the Prince of Wales – whose name was
                                        Frederick Louis,
Was hit upon the head, and so his legs went soft and gooey.
He later died because he got that bouncer to the brain,
So in his case you might say the result was 'play stopped reign'.

RICHARD STILGOE, from song entitled 'The Prince of Wales'.

FOR all his brilliance and beauty and strength he was increasingly distressed by the very fast stuff. It might have been to do with the drinking bouts, rare but increasingly fast and furious, the 'mild' drug addiction, the sex-drive and a progressively disturbed mental and emotional condition.

TEST KILL, written by Ted Dexter and Clifford Makins, on why England's No 3 felt obliged to murder Australia's terrifying fast bowler.

A Note on Sources

The authors would like to express their thanks and indebtedness to all the works quoted in this book, particularly the following which provided such a rich source of information:

Bat and Ball, edited by Thomas Moult, (Sportsman's Press, 1956)
The Cricketer's Companion, edited by Alan Ross, (Eyre Methuen, 1979)
A History of Cricket, H. S. Altham, (Allen and Unwin, 1929)
The Jubilee Book of Cricket, Ranjitsinhji, (Blackwood, 1897)
Recollections and Reminiscences, Lord Hawke, (Williams and Norgate, 1922)
The Willow Wand, Derek Birley (Queen Anne Press, 1979)

The various works of Mike Brearley, Neville Cardus, Jack Fingleton, R. C. Robertson-Glasgow, Peter Roebuck and the files of the *Cricketer* and *Wisden Cricket Monthly* have also proved invaluable and deserve special thanks.

Index